Everything you need to know to get started

TELEVISION PROGRAM MAKING

Everything you need to know to get started

COLIN HART

Illustrations by CHRIS MUTTER

Focal Press

OXFORD AUCKLAND BOSTON JOHANNESBURG MELBOURNE NEW DELHI

Focal Press
An imprint of Butterworth-Heinemann
Linacre House, Jordan Hill, Oxford OX2 8DP
225 Wildwood Avenue, Woburn, MA 01801-2041
A division of Reed Educational and Professional Publishing Ltd

A member of the Reed Elsevier plc group

First published 1999

British Library Cataloguing in Publication Data
A catalogue record for this book is available from the British Library

Library of Congress Cataloguing in Publication Data
A catalogue record for this book is available from the Library of Congress

ISBN 0 240 51524 2

Printed and bound in Great Britain by
Biddles Ltd, Guildford and King's Lynn

FOR EVERY TITLE THAT WE PUBLISH, BUTTERWORTH-HEINEMANN
WILL PAY FOR BTCV TO PLANT AND CARE FOR A TREE.

CONTENTS

Contents

condensing action – punctuation – split edits – cutting to music –
making it fit – learning from the edit.

Chapter 16 – Online Editing   187

2D and 3D effects – using DVE – planning effects – image effects –
estimating online time.

Chapter 17 – Post-production Sound   193

The dubbing process – recording voice-over – repairing, improving
and editing – adding music – foreign language dubs – subtitling.

Chapter 18 – Sample Productions   202

News – current affairs – corporate video – drama.

Chapter 19 – Working as a Freelance   212

Why go freelance? – finding work – marketing yourself – deciding
your rate – administration – getting paid – choosing an accountant
– book-keeping basics – VAT.

Chapter 20 – Good Housekeeping   222

Keeping track of tapes – maintaining a showreel – contacts –
music – budgets – trade press.

Chapter 21 – Shooting and Editing on Film   225

The shoot – processing and transfers – editing on film – editing
on film and tape.

Chapter 22 – Further Information   230

Trade magazines, directories and organisations.

Glossary   236

Common technical terms, abbreviations, slang and jargon.

Index   251

Acknowledgments

A number of people have helped in the preparation of this book: Derek Oliver of ESP Facilities who reminded me what happens on a multi-camera shoot, Tony Appleton of Fairline Post Production who helped with the editing chapters and Jon Walley of TVP who brought me up to date on tape formats. Any errors or inaccuracies are entirely of my making, not theirs. My thanks also to everyone at OpTex and Sennheiser for their assistance with picture references.

My thanks as well to Joy Mutter for her work on the layout and to Chris Mutter for his illustrations. Finally, my thanks to my life partner, Angie Littler, whose idea this was, for her advice, support and tolerance.

Colin Hart
Suffolk

Introduction

Who this book is for

This book is for anyone starting out or hoping to work in the ever-expanding world of television and video. Everyone involved in a TV or video production is contributing to the program making process. They all need to know and understand how it happens. Whatever you want to end up doing, whether you are part way through a course or starting from scratch, this book gives you all the essential information you will need.

You may want to work in television, in commercials, in corporate video, pop promos or maybe move around between all of them. You may see yourself as a producer, a director, a camera operator or a set designer. You may choose to work in sport, news, documentaries, game shows or drama. Wherever you work and whatever you are doing, the basic principles are going to be the same. And you'll save yourself a lot of sleepless nights if you know them and understand them.

Why do you want to work in this industry?

It's glamorous, it's fun, you get to travel, you meet famous people, it opens doors that are closed to most people, you can wear what you like, the work is varied, the money's not bad, the women are pretty and some of the men are even prettier.

These of course are not the reasons that motivate most people, though they happen by and large to be true. The downside is that it is hard work, both mentally and physically. It isn't always that good for your health. You'll suffer long periods of boredom followed by frantic moments of intense activity. It's not a 9 to 5 business, it's not predictable and in most jobs there is no set routine. But if you're a bit of a neurotic and don't fancy life shifting paper from an in-tray to an out-tray, you're probably right for the business.

Is this you?

You need to be the kind of person who can think quickly but not too deeply. You need to want to know about the world around you. You will need what the trainers call good 'interpersonal' skills. This means getting on with people. You'll almost always be working with other people as part of a team, often under pressure. Productions go much better if you're not all at one another's throats.

A sense of humour helps. So does a sense of what makes a good picture, of what makes a good story and of what other people will be interested in watching and listening to on the screen. That doesn't just apply to directors. Sound recordists might have the best equipment and record the purest sound but if they don't have a sense of what is going on and the mike isn't pointing at the right person at the right time, they might just as well not be there.

You will need a good memory. However detailed your notes or script, there'll be times when you can't consult them and you'll have to remember what you do next. However good your log is, and even with playback, you still need to remember what you did yesterday so that it fits with what you are doing today.

Part of the attraction of the business is that it appears to be conducted in an atmosphere of happy chaos. Don't be fooled. Like a lot of the work that is being produced, this is a carefully crafted illusion. Very little would ever get done if it was really like that. The reality is that you need to be well organised and punctual, able to work on your own initiative and prepared to shoulder responsibility.

You will always go on learning

You will never know it all. You will always go on learning. If you don't know something, don't pretend you do. There's always someone to ask and they'll usually enjoy telling you (provided you're up to speed on those all important interpersonal skills).

If you want to know more, there are plenty more books to read. But there's one other thing you can do. Watch loads of television.

Once you've read the book, completed your training and are making your own programs, keep watching what other people are doing.

Knowing what you now know, you'll soon be able to spot the multi-camera from the single camera shoots. On a live discussion program, why did the director cut to a particular reaction shot? Was it because it was interesting or was it just an escape shot? How did they get that tracking shot – was it using an expensive jib-arm on a dolly or did they lash the camera to a skateboard?

Then ask yourself – How Would I Do That?

Chapter 1
An Overview

Whatever kind of program you are making, you are always making it for someone else to watch. That is, unless you have unlimited personal funds and think it's fun to make programs only you will watch. In which case, thanks for buying the book, but you're not going to get a lot out of it.

The Audience Comes First

Successful program makers are always thinking about their audience. At every stage you should be asking yourself:

- who is this aimed at?
- will it interest them?
- will it hold their attention?
- will they enjoy watching it?
- is it delivering information they want, or ideas and messages that you want them to receive?

The audience comes first. The type of audience will determine the kind of program you are making and the way you decide to make it.

There's always a 'Client'

There will always be someone sitting between you and the audience – the client. In broadcast television the client is the program editor or commissioning editor. In corporate video the client could be the company executive who has ordered the work plus any of their external advisers who are involved in the project. Similarly, with commercials you will have both the corporate client and their advertising agency. If you are making a music video, your clients could include the band, their manager, the record company, PR people, merchandisers and marketeers.

Clients can be a pain. But at the end of the day, or sometimes well after it, they are paying you to do the job. Just occasionally they have as good an idea as you think you have of what will work with the end-audience and what will not. So you need to listen to your client. As well as thinking about whether your ideas are going to work with the audience, you have to think about whether the client is going to buy them.

Clients are seldom program makers. That's why they're employing you. But if they know their own business they know what audiences want. Clients can be a valuable filter between you – with your creative ideas – and the end-audience who may not actually be quite ready for your singular approach. So making a program to please the client isn't quite as creepy as it sounds. If you get the relationship right and there's a positive exchange of ideas between the two of you, the end result can be the better for it.

Let's assume you have got off on the right foot with your client and they want you to make a program or you have come to them with an idea. Where do you start and what is likely to happen?

The Process

The program-making process can be broken down into five key stages:

- **Development**
- **Pre-production**
- **Production**
- **Post-production**
- **Clearing up**

Development

A program is in development while it is being thought about, talked about and costed. It will involve you having an idea, researching it, thinking about how to translate it onto the screen, writing it up as a treatment, drawing up a budget and selling the concept to your client.

Pre-production

Once the program has been commissioned you move into pre-production. You will be carrying out more research, selecting locations, talking to people who may appear in the program, choosing a presenter or actors, writing a shooting script, drawing up storyboards and planning the production schedule. You might also be designing sets, selecting props and costumes, viewing library footage or clearing copyright on music.

Unless you are going to do everything yourself, you will also be selecting the team that will be working with you. You will need to book them for the days you will need them and possibly make sure they are fed, watered and transported. Careful pre-production is essential. Get it right and your production stands a good chance of going smoothly and to budget. Get it wrong and you could end up with an expensive shambles.

Production

You are now ready to move into production. You start to shoot or acquire material. This is also known as the acquisition stage.

Post-production

With shooting completed you move into post-production. You start to edit, usually completing a low resolution offline edit first. Once that has been approved by your client, you will make any changes, record the final commentary and complete a high resolution online assembly adding any visual effects. Depending on the equipment you are using and the complexity of your sound tracks you may be able to mix the sound in the online assembly. If not, you will take your finished master tape into a sound dubbing theatre to add the finishing touches.

Clearing Up

Finally, there is clearing up. You may need to arrange for duplication if copies of the program are needed. There may be thank-you letters to be written, publicity to be organised, bills to be paid and money to be got in. There'll be some accountancy – were you on budget, under it or over it? You will have accumulated a lot of paperwork along the way. You have to decide what to chuck and what to file and where. The same goes for all the tapes you have used.

That is an overview of the five key stages to any production. Each is dealt with in more detail later. Those five stages could take place over any period of time. A major drama series could be several years in development while a news story is often planned, shot, edited and transmitted within a matter of hours. Whatever the production, the sequence of events is always the same. But don't imagine one stage will be fully completed before you move onto the next. They have a habit of running into one another and overlapping. You might need to start to editing one part of a program before you start shooting another part. You may well find that your script is changing throughout the process.

What You Will Need

Development and Pre-production

In the development and pre-production stages all you will need in the way of equipment is a desk, telephone, pen, paper, files and folders, an address book, a diary and, ideally, a personal computer with word processing and spreadsheet software. You are also likely to need some means of transport.

Production

Once you are in production and start to shoot you will obviously need a camera and tape stock. The type of camera you use will depend on the tape format you are shooting on. The lowest cost option is **VHS**. The standard professional tape format for most broadcast and corporate work is **Betacam SP** (known as Beta SP).

If you are looking for even better picture quality you could shoot on **Digital Betacam** (known as Digibeta) but equipment, tape stock and subsequent editing will all cost more. A less expensive digital option is the **DV** format which ranks below Beta SP but which nonetheless can give acceptable results.

Post-production

When you have completed your shoot and you are in post-production, you will probably carry out two major edits of your program – an **offline** and an **online**. In essence the offline edit is a low-resolution edit that gives you a chance to play with all the material and see if it works. Once you and your client are happy, the program is finally assembled and visual effects are added in the online edit. Your completed program is known as the **edit master**.

For the offline edit you have two choices. You can either do the whole job on tape using one or more playback machines linked to a record machine or you can use a digital desktop system. For the online edit you have three choices. You can online on a standard linear tape system, on a digital tape system, or on a digital desktop system. All of these options are explored in more detail in Chapter 14.

If you are going to be including any **graphics** in your program, there are a variety of different ways you can generate them. The old-fashioned method – and it still works – is to have them created by hand and then shoot them under a **rostrum camera**. You would also use a rostrum camera to shoot any other artwork or still pictures. However, most TV graphics today are created on dedicated high-end computer workstations which then output to tape. Alternatively, you can use standard PC or Mac graphics software but the results may not be quite so good and you need to be sure your editing equipment can read the disks and computer files you will be creating. There is a fuller explanation of graphics systems in Chapter 13.

The **soundtrack** of your program is likely to be made up of a number of elements: voice-over commentary, music, sound effects and of course the sound you have recorded with the pictures you have shot. These all need to be mixed on the final track of your edit master. Sometimes this can be done at the online edit. If the sound is at all complicated, it is often better to complete it in what is known as a **sound suite** or **dubbing theatre**.

In summary you are likely to need:

- Camera equipment

- Offline edit suite

- Online edit suite

- Graphics workstation

- Sound suite

These are all known as **facilities**. If you are working for a TV station all of the technical facilities you need will probably be in-house. If not, there is no need to rush out and buy them all. They can all be hired. Camera equipment is normally hired by the day. Everything else can normally be hired by the hour.

Who You Will Need

There are six key roles that have to be performed for any production:

Producer –

ultimately responsible for all aspects of the production – creative, administrative, logistical, legal and financial.

Director –

leads and supervises all shooting and editing, makes sure it happens, makes sure it looks good and sounds good, makes sure it works.

Scriptwriter –

develops the initial concept, creates the basic structure of the program and writes the commentary.

Camera operator –

operates the camera and is responsible for technical quality of pictures.

Sound recordist –

responsible for recording sound.

Offline editor –

edits program working closely with the director.

Online editor –

assembles final edit master and adds visual effects.

In theory one person can fulfill all of those tasks. But two heads are better than one and mistakes can happen if you are trying to rewrite the script, operate the camera, check the background and deliver a piece to camera all on your own.

If you are working for a TV station, all of the people needed may be in-house. If not, they can all be hired. Very often camera equipment and crew will come together as a package. Similarly, editors and their equipment can be hired with one phone call.

The television industry is highly fragmented. It consists of thousands of freelances and hundreds of facility companies all eager to work. So don't be put off by the thought that you need to invest in lots of expensive equipment before you can start making programs.

Tape Formats

At a very early stage – certainly when you are drawing up the budget – you will need to decide on the tape format you are going to shoot on and the system you will be using for editing. The decision may be made partly for you. If you are producing a program for broadcast, the TV station will set a quality standard you have to meet. For example, they may say that all shooting must be on Beta SP or above and the program must be mastered to D3. If you are shooting a corporate program your choice of format will be dictated by the budget available and the quality level the client is used to.

To understand the difference between the various types of film and tape formats you are likely to be shooting and editing on, it is worth spending a moment on the history and prehistory of television.

A Little Bit of History

Television has only been around for the past 50 years. Don't ask what people did before then. It doesn't bear thinking about. Before then, if you wanted to record moving images, the only way to do it was on film and the only way you could show people your film was via a projector onto a screen. The audience had to come to the picture house or you had to take your projector to them.

Television meant that film could be transmitted over the airwaves and viewed on a receiver in the home. But television didn't just transmit films. It also transmitted images via the newly-invented electronic camera. In the early days these images were always 'live' images for the very good reason that no one had invented a satisfactory means of recording the output of the electronic camera.

The TV producer's choice was a bit limited. A drama shot in the studio using electronic cameras had to be shot live. What you saw in your home was actually happening in front of the cameras in the studio – complete with actors fluffing or forgetting their lines and the director getting the cameras tied up in knots round one another. If the script called for a sequence to be shot outside the studio – on location – it had to be shot on film, edited and then the package played into the transmission at the appropriate moment.

Electronic TV cameras could be taken out of the studio and used on location for an outside broadcast but as its name implies this was always for live coverage of a live event. The cameras were fairly hefty pieces of equipment and operated from static, fixed positions. The advantage over film, though, was first that the viewer saw the event as it happened and second, it could be viewed from a number of different angles. There is virtually no limit to the number of cameras you can use on an outside broadcast.

In the 1960s life got a little easier with the development of VTR (video tape recording). Now you could record the output of electronic TV cameras onto 2" magnetic tape on a machine the size of three fridges. Less and less television was live. But because of the size of electronic camera equipment all location shooting continued to be on film.

That all changed in the 1980s with the arrival of ENG (electronic news gathering) video cameras. Roughly the same size and weight as 16mm film cameras, they can operate with lower light levels and because they record onto magnetic tape, you are saved the time and cost of film stock processing. ENG systems became particularly popular with news and current affairs producers, for whom time is a key factor, and with corporate producers looking to minimise costs.

There are now two types of tape – linear and digital. With **linear** or **analogue** tape, sound and pictures are recorded frame by frame – in much the same way as on a strip of film, except that you can't hold it up to the light and look at the pictures. To edit, you have to re-record the shots you want, one at a time in the sequence you want them from playback machines. There is a slight loss of picture quality in the process and making changes is time-consuming.

The breakthrough of the 1990s has been the arrival of **digital** formats for both shooting and editing. Sound and picture information is stored digitally on tape in much the same way as it is encoded and stored on a computer disk. This gives superior picture quality which is maintained throughout the editing process and means that editing itself has become much more flexible.

Despite these advances many producers still shoot on a linear tape format and then edit on a combination of linear and digital systems. For the very best quality, shooting on film is still many people's preferred option. If this all seems a bit confusing at first, don't worry. It all gets simpler once you start to do it. The options open to you are explored in more detail in Chapter 14.

So that's the background to where we are today. In some ways life is a lot simpler than it was when television began. In other ways it has become more complex. Tape and equipment manufacturers are all trying to steal a march on one another by bringing out a succession of different formats, each hoping theirs will be the one that scoops the pool. As a result there is a host of different formats around.

Linear Tape Formats

These are the principal linear tape formats you could be shooting on. They are listed in descending order of quality.

1 inch

fast becoming obsolete; was the standard format for edit mastering.

Betacam SP

usually referred to as Beta SP, the standard linear format for most broadcast news, current affairs, documentary and corporate shooting.

Betacam

predecessor of the above.

Hi-band umatic

was the corporate standard but seldom used now.

Lo-band umatic

was used for low-budget corporate productions and still used for some offline editing.

Hi8

superior domestic system.

SVHS

superior domestic system still used for linear offline editing.

VHS

domestic only or for duplication copies.

Digital Tape Formats

Digital tape formats for shooting are:

Digital betacam

usually referred to as Digibeta, high quality equivalent to Super 16 film and increasingly used on drama and even commercials.

DVCPro, DVCam, Digital S & Beta SX

slightly below linear Beta SP quality but watch this space.

D1, D2, D3, D5

mainly used for edit mastering. There is no D4 because it sounds like the word for 'death' in Japanese.

Film Formats

35mm

very high quality, very expensive, almost only ever used for cinema features and commercials.

Super 16

used mainly on drama shoots and quality documentaries when the budget won't stretch to 35mm.

16mm

was the pre-tape broadcast standard, now largely overtaken by Super 16.

Worldwide Television Systems

Tape formats are universal. A roll of Beta SP tape bought in Tokyo will be the same as one purchased in London or San Francisco. But there is no single worldwide standard for television equipment such as cameras, recorders, playback machines and monitors. There are three different standards. These are NTSC, PAL and SECAM.

If you are shooting outside your home country, using library material from another country or making copies to be shown abroad, you need to check what standard is used where.

NTSC is the standard system for the United States and Japan.

PAL was developed in Great Britain where it is the standard. It is also found in much of western Europe and former British colonies.

SECAM was developed in France where it is the standard. It is also the standard for Russia, much of eastern Europe and the former French colonies.

So if you are British producer wanting to shoot on tape in France using a locally-based crew you have one of two choices. Either find a crew that has PAL equipment or shoot on SECAM and then get the tapes converted to the PAL standard once you are back home. **Standards conversion** is an additional cost. You will also have to accept some loss of quality. NTSC and SECAM are in any case inherently inferior to PAL.

If you are shooting on film there is no need to worry about TV standards. Film formats are universally the same. It is only when your film gets onto tape that you will need to think about it.

If you need to make copies of a program to be shown outside your home country, it is advisable to check on the TV standard for that country. Any reputable duplication house that also does standards conversion will be able to tell you the right standard for any country.

Film

We are going to assume throughout most of this book that you are shooting and editing on tape. However, there may be occasions when you want to shoot on film. For example, most high quality drama is shot on film. Shooting on film is more expensive than shooting on tape. Film stock costs more than tape, lighting is more critical and you will need a specialist film camera operator usually with an assistant. Exposed film has to be processed and editing on film can take longer than a tape edit. Very often program makers shoot on film and then transfer the rushes to tape for editing; again an additional cost. If you can make the case for shooting on film and persuade a client to pay for it, you will find a fuller description of what is involved in Chapter 21.

Chapter 2
Who Does What?

In this chapter we will be looking at how television programs get to be made, who commissions them, who pays for them and who makes them. We will be looking at how the industry is organised, the different types of company involved and the various roles that individuals play. Most of this is described in the context of the UK television industry.

The Sectors

The industry can be divided into two sectors: **broadcast** and **non-broadcast**.

The broadcast sector is television as we all know and watch it most days in our homes – news, documentaries, sport, drama and entertainment packaged into a schedule.

The non-broadcast sector is better known as video – programs made for training, for internal company communication, for sales, marketing and promotion. The non-broadcast sector also includes training, education and special interest videos made for hire or sale. There is considerable crossover between the two sectors. Many people work in both in the course of their careers or even from day to day. A freelance camera operator could be working on a TV game show one day and on a corporate video for a car manufacturer the next.

Key People

In both the broadcast and the non-broadcast sector, there are four types of person or organisation involved in making a program; the commissioner or **client** who wants a program made and who has the money to do it, the **producer** or production company who will see the job through to completion and the **freelances** and **facilities** that the producer will employ to get the work done.

Traditionally, in large broadcast organisations all of those people or functions were under one roof. In recent years that has been changing. Channel 4 produces almost no programs itself. It acts more as a publisher, inviting ideas from independent program makers and then funding their production. The BBC and ITV are now obliged by law to commission a percentage of their output from independents. At the same time the BBC actively encourages its own producers to use external facilities. In turn, the BBC and the ITV companies offer their own technical facilities for hire to independent producers. In theory, an independent producer could be making a program for the BBC, using a freelance camera operator with equipment hired from an independent hire company, shooting in HTV's studios and editing at ITN. This is not the recommended method but it demonstrates how fragmented the industry has become.

The Broadcasters

In most countries the broadcast sector is dominated by major corporations transmitting programs direct into people's homes. There are three ways of doing that:

- by using land-based transmitters (terrestrial)

- via satellite

- by cable.

Terrestrial broadcasters still continue to produce a high proportion of the programs they transmit, using their own staff and facilities; but far less than they used to. Increasingly, they commission programs from independent producers or production companies.

Satellite broadcasters produce almost nothing themselves apart from news programs. Everything else is bought in – from terrestrial broadcasters, film studios or independent producers. Satellite broadcasters may buy the rights to television coverage of a sports event but will probably contract out the actual production.

Cable companies are also primarily distributors of other people's work rather than originators of programs. Exceptions are shopping channels and news channels; but again, much of their news material may have been bought in from agencies.

What this all means for program makers and technicians is that there are fewer opportunities for full-time permanent jobs with the broadcasters. Even when the broadcasters are making a program in-house, staff will tend to be employed on short-term contracts. The upside is that there are more opportunities for people to do their own thing, to make the programs they want to make and not be constricted by the demands of a large, bureaucratic organisation. That's the theory, anyway. First you have got to persuade the broadcasters that you have got the ideas, the talent and the ability that they think they are looking for. You will also have to accept that permanent jobs are a thing of the past.

Production Companies

The changes in the way the industry operates have led to the rise and rise of independent production companies. A production company can consist of no more than one producer and a telephone. The producer will sell an idea to a broadcaster or a corporate client, put together the team that is needed to make the program and then see the production through to completion.

As a general rule, production companies will wait until they have got a commitment and funding before making a program. There are exceptions to this. Some production companies are effectively video publishers. Using their own or investors' money they will make programs which they then hope to hire out or sell either to companies or the general public.

A successful production company needs to combine a degree of creativity with sound business management skills. A good producer needs to be able to recognise good ideas and foster creative talent. At the same time a producer must be able to manage financial and technical resources efficiently.

The word 'production' conjures up an image of machines and

equipment churning out a product.

In fact, few production companies own all or any of the technical facilities they may need. They are also unlikely to employ full-time staff to make their programs. Camera kit and editing equipment are expensive. They need to be working all the time to pay for themselves. So most independent producers will go to specialist facilities and hire in cameras, studios, editing, graphics and sound dubbing. The people that are needed will either come with the facility or will be freelances hired on a day-to-day or project basis. Writers and directors also tend to be hired on a freelance basis.

Facilities

In Britain the best and widest choice of facilities is to be found in London's Soho but you will usually find adequate post-production facilities wherever you are. The same applies to camera crews and equipment. There are professionals dotted around everywhere and producers will often save on hotel and travel costs by picking up locally-based crews wherever they plan to shoot throughout the world. However, this can be a false economy. You are less likely to achieve the shooting style you want from a camera operator you are working with for the first time. That can also be true for editing. Anyone can set up as a camera operator, designer or editor. There are few recognised diplomas or qualifications. So you need to check out what people have done before, their level of experience and the clients they have worked for.

Finding the right facilities is a matter of trial, error and word of mouth. Facilities advertise themselves in the trade magazines and are listed in trade directories. A number of these are listed in Chapter 22. Magazines and directories are a good starting point but, whenever you can, talk to someone else who has used a facility you are thinking of using for the first time.

There are several different ways of hiring facilities. With **dry-hire** a producer hires equipment or a studio and then brings in their own people or their preferred freelances. This way they get exactly the people they want but there is a lot more work involved; more telephoning around beforehand, more book-keeping and more cheques to be written afterwards. Not surprisingly, most producers go for packages – a camera crew and all equipment or a studio complete with all the people and equipment needed to operate it. Alternatively, a producer might bring in one or two preferred people and leave the facility to supply the rest. The choice is theirs.

People

The television industry glories in a host of different job titles. Some of these are fairly self-evident. Others are incomprehensible to outsiders. Broadly speaking, the television world divides into two types of person – production and technical. It is very easy to tell them apart. Production people never carry anything heavier than a clipboard or a mobile phone. They are all part of the Production Team and tell everyone else what to do. Everyone else is generally referred to as The Crew, except for editors, designers, writers and composers. No one is ever quite sure whether they are Crew or Production. If this suggests the class system is alive and well in television, you wouldn't be so very wrong.

In the past the industry was heavily unionised and there were clear demarcation lines between different jobs. Today there is a greater degree of flexibility. On different productions and in different companies, functions and job descriptions can vary. The list below is a general guide to the main jobs people perform and what is commonly understood by the job title.

Production Team

Executive Producer

Usually does very little. Might have come up with the original idea or more likely the finance. Could be the MD of the production company or the series editor in charge of a string of programs being produced by a number of producers. Probably keeps a watching eye on how the production is going and whether it is on budget – between long lunches.

Producer

Ultimately responsible for all aspects of an individual production – creative, administrative, logistical, legal and financial. Primarily a team builder, choosing and hiring key personnel and facilities. Answerable to the executive producer.

Director

In creative charge of the production – leads and supervises all shooting and editing, makes sure it happens, makes sure it looks good and sounds good, makes sure it works. Answerable to the producer but a wise producer who has chosen well leaves the director to get on with it.

The extent to which the director is the 'author' of a production is a subject of endless debate. Much will depend on how a production has been originally conceived and at what stage the director has become involved.

Assistant Director

AD deputises for the director on location shoots. Tasks will vary and could include selecting and setting up locations, liaising with props, costume, set designer and casting. Might direct extras for crowd scenes.

Art Director

Usually only on commercials – comes up with the concept and visual ideas which are then made to happen by the director.

Scriptwriter

Writes the treatment, devises the structure of a program, suggests the visual content and writes dialogue and commentary. Usually briefed by and answerable to the producer. May work closely with the director or the two might never meet.

On commercials the art director and scriptwriter (or copywriter) will tend to be in-house staff of an advertising agency taking their brief from a client. Together they will devise a detailed concept which is then briefed out to the production company who will actually make the commercial.

Production Manager

A catch-all title for whoever fixes, arranges and organises everything. Answerable to the producer but works closely with the director. Responsible for all logistics, travel, accommodation, feeding and watering. Hires freelance technicians, equipment and facilities, negotiating rates and terms. May be responsible for drawing up and monitoring the budget on behalf of the producer, might carry out initial recces for the director and scout for locations. A good production manager thinks ahead all the time, anticipating what the producer and director might need.

Production Assistant

Ensures that the shooting script is updated, followed and logged. Usually responsible for continuity on the shoot, ensuring that shots match and will cut together. Logs all takes and marks them against the script. May also perform other secretarial functions and double as a production manager.

Technical Crew

Lighting Director

Helps the director achieve the visual effect required by co-ordinating the work of the camera operator and the lighting electricians.

Camera Operator

Operates the camera and is responsible for the technical quality of pictures. Often acts as lighting director and may carry and set own lights.

Camera Assistant

Carries and sets up camera equipment. A relative luxury on video shoots but essential on film shoots where a second person is needed to load and discharge the magazine.

Sound Recordist

Responsible for recording sound.

Sound Assistant

Works as part of the recordist's team setting, monitoring or operating a microphone such as a boom mike.

Electrician

Sets and adjusts lights under the direction of the lighting director or camera operator. Known as a **Spark**. Where a team of sparks is needed, the chief electrician is known as the **Gaffer** and the number two as the **Best Boy**.

Grip

A general term for anyone who carries camera equipment and sets it up. In particular, the grip sets track and operates tracking equipment.

On a multi-camera shoot other key personnel are:

Vision Mixer

Cuts between each camera's output selecting the final transmission picture. In North America is known as the **Switcher**.

Vision Controller

Monitors and adjusts picture quality of each camera's output. Also known as 'racks'.

Sound Supervisor

Operates sound mixing desk and directs sound crew.

Floor Manager

Controls all movement and activity on the studio floor. Communicates director's requirements to everyone working on the studio floor and is the link between the director and on-camera talent such as presenters, actors and interviewees.

In addition, a production might need the services of:

Casting Director

Selects potential actors and arranges auditions.

Designer

Designs sets and supervises their construction.

Graphics Designer

Designs and creates title sequence and any graphics included in the program.

Properties Buyer

Usually referred to as 'props', the person who selects and assembles any miscellaneous items required for the shoot. Any inanimate object that is not part of the set but which will appear on camera is a **prop** – a book, a box of matches, a cup and saucer, etc.

Stylist

Arranges props or product packs to best visual effect.

Costume

Selects, hires or buys all clothing to be worn by on-camera artists.

Make-Up Artist

One of the few job titles that needs no explanation.

Runner

On a location shoot runs errands. In a facility does the same plus making sure clients are regularly topped up with coffee, pizzas, etc. A great way into the business: 'Never be rude to the runner – could be your boss one day.'

Once a program moves into post-production, key individuals are the **offline editor**, the **online editor** and the **dubbing mixer**. Their roles are described more fully in the chapters on Editing and Post-production Sound.

Chapter 3
The Treatment

As we saw in Chapter 1 all programs are made for an audience. Sitting between the audience and the producer is the client. Your client could be a TV channel commissioner, a corporate organisation, a record company, an advertising agency, a program editor or a tutor.

Your client will want to know your thinking, how you will approach the production and how it is likely to look on the screen. That's what a treatment is all about. It is a selling document. But it also helps you to sort out your thoughts on paper. So even though there's no cast-iron rule that says you have to write a treatment before you can start shooting, it's worth doing even if no one else is actually demanding it.

Research

Before you start writing the treatment you will need to do some research. This may have been done partly for you if you have been given a brief. Even so, you will want to know whether the ideas you have in mind can actually be put into practice. There may be aspects of the brief you don't fully understand. Does what you think you want to shoot actually exist? Who are the people you might want to interview? What sort of locations and subjects are there to shoot?

If possible, go and talk to people and get a feel of the locations and the subject. You should be looking for two things: people who talk well and will give good interviews and subjects that will be visually interesting. Getting out and doing some research will also give you ideas about how you are going to tackle the subject. It will help you decide on the program format that will work best and give you ideas for bringing it to life on the screen.

Writing the Treatment

Writing the treatment is a lot easier if you organise your thoughts and ideas under a number of headings.

Treatment Checklist

These are the headings you could use to draw up a treatment:

- ☐ The brief or the idea
- ☐ Target audience
- ☐ Style of production
- ☐ Creative approach
- ☐ Structure and content
- ☐ Storyboard
- ☐ Technical
- ☐ Credentials
- ☐ Budget

Example

A treatment for a fund-raising video to be made for a children's charity.

The Brief

You state in a few words what the video is intended to achieve.

This treatment is for a video to be produced on behalf of a leading children's charity. It will be used as part of the charity's ongoing fundraising efforts.

Target Audience

Who will actually see the video? Who is it meant to influence and what do they need to be told? It is very important to get this clear from the outset. A video aimed at people who work full-time for the charity could be very different in tone and content from one aimed at potential donors.

> The primary audience will be potential donors. They will have some knowledge of the work of the charity but this needs to be developed. While the video will be making an emotional appeal and drawing attention to the plight of children whom the charity aims to help, it must also satisfy potential donors that the charity is in fact capable of addressing their needs and does so in both a caring and cost-efficient manner.

By defining the audience, you have already begun to define what the video has to show and probably the order in which it will do it.

Style of Production

Now you need to decide what kind of video you plan to produce. Is it going to be a mini-documentary, a journalistic report? Will it be shot on location or in a studio? Will it have a presenter? Will it have a voice-over or will you allow the story to be told in a series of soundbites from people you interview? If it was a training video, you might want to shoot it as a drama.

Your client may have their own ideas about how it should be done and you may need to convince them that your approach is the right one. The budget you have available may also influence your decision on the style of the production. This is a non-broadcast program so it may be worth relating the type of production you have to one that your client is already familiar with from broadcast television.

> We have considered a number of alternatives as to what style of production is appropriate. We feel that shooting the video in a studio and interviewing senior officers of the charity would lack emotional impact and would not give the

audience a full picture of the work the charity does. The audience needs to see the children who are being helped, to hear from them and to see how in a practical way the charity meets their needs.

There are considerable advantages to having the video fronted by a well-known presenter, as this will add to the credibility of the messages. However, this has cost implications, even if the presenter is working for less than their normal fee in this case.

We therefore propose a production that is shot entirely on location with the commentary delivered voice-over by a narrator. The main editorial messages would be delivered by senior officers of the charity through excerpts from interviews. Wherever possible we shall illustrate what is being said with live action sequences showing the children and the work the charity is doing for them. On the screen the finished production will have the look and feel of a report that people would expect to see as part of a broadcast television current affairs program. It would have a running time of no more than 10 minutes.

Both you and your client now have a clear idea of the type of production to expect. You have also given persuasive reasons for not making either a studio-based or presenter-led program.

Creative Approach

In this case you have in fact largely described your creative approach in the section headed Style of Production. But you might want to say something about how you are going to shoot various sequences and the effect you are aiming to achieve.

Children are naturally appealing photographic subjects and, as such, are at their best when seen at their most natural. Whenever shooting the children we shall adopt a fly-on-the-wall approach, letting them be themselves as we capture images that the audience will immediately respond to.

While most of the program will consist of rapportage, we shall also use music, particularly in the closing sequences, to reinforce the emotional appeal of the message.

The scripted voice-over narration will be written in an objective style using as few words as possible, serving principally as a link between soundbites from children, carers and key officials of the charity. We shall not script any of the interviews. People will be allowed to speak naturally and spontaneously. When we come to edit we shall use the clips that best help tell the story.

This last paragraph is important. You need to make clear how you are going to handle the verbal content of the program – the voice-over and the interviews.

Structure and Content

To some extent you are now starting to write the outline of the script. If someone else is actually going to write the script, they will need this section, though they may not stick to it. Nor will you probably, but it gives you a good basis for what you will be aiming to do later.

You should go into some detail in this section but if you are writing the treatment for someone else to read, try not to let it become too technical. Above all, write it from the point of view of the audience. You're not producing this video for yourself. You are producing it for a specific audience. Put yourself in their position. Stand back and look at the program as they will. Just by doing this, you should be able to get a sense of whether the production is going to work even at this early stage.

Sequence 1

Opening title featuring animation of the charity's logo backed by classical music – gentle violin (e.g. Bach's Where Sheep May Safely Graze)

Sequence 2

Music continues as we mix to a shot of a small girl sitting on the grass picking daisies. Beside her is her teddy bear. As she picks the daisies she puts them in a cup and talks to the teddy bear.

We hear the voice of one of the charity's carers. She starts to tell us the little girl's story. Her name is Karen. She had been mistreated and is now looked after by the charity. The audience are immediately aware of the contrast between the girl's former life and the scene we see now. As the carer speaks, we continue to see Karen talking to her teddy bear.

Sequence 3

We cut to a day room full of children playing and the voice-over explains that Karen is just one of forty children cared for in this home.

We now see the carer talking in interview with the children in the background. She tells us of the different backgrounds the children have come from...

That is just a flavour of how you might write the Structure and Content section. It's the foundation of your script but it is not laid out as the script will be. You will probably notice in the example above that you are doing several things at once. You are describing the pictures, the voice track, the music and the effect you want to achieve with the audience. When you come to write it as a script, the technique is quite different.

Programs are built up as a series of sequences. A sequence is a series of shots that tell an aspect of the story. In the example above we have described the first three sequences. In a full treatment you might want to describe the whole program in this way.

This section of the treatment will demonstrate several things:

* you already have a clear idea of the structure of the program

* you understand and have a feel for the subject matter

* you understand the audience and what will work best with them

* you have thought about how you are going to combine the spoken word, live action shots, special effects, graphics, ambient sound and recorded music to achieve an overall effect.

Remember, too, that most people have a hard time visualising what they are going to see and hear on the screen. Your treatment needs to take them through it step by step and you need to choose words and terms they will readily understand.

Storyboard

Very often words alone will not be enough and you will need to storyboard a sequence. A storyboard is a bit like a comic strip. You draw key frames in a sequence and below them describe what is happening visually and what is being heard on the soundtrack.

Action: Woman walks down night time street.

VO:
You know how it is.

Action: Woman turns and enters brightly lit shop front.

VO:
When you need some help.

Action: Woman inside shop speaking to unseen character.

WOMAN:
'Sir, I'm in trouble.'

Action: Private eye emerges from shadows.

VO:
She'd come to the ...

Action: Reverse angle shot as she gazes at her saviour.

VO:
... right place.

Action: Closer shot of woman.

WOMAN:
'I'm so glad I found you.'

Storyboards are often the only way of showing how an animation or title sequence is going to work.

Technical

Depending on the budget and equipment available to you, you should specify what tape format you will be shooting on and mastering to. It is also worth mentioning the editing system you will be using and how any graphics will be generated.

Credentials

You need to sell yourself as well as your ideas. Programs are made by people. Your client will want to know about your program-making experience, your credits, and the credentials of the team you will be working with. Tell them about your own previous productions, particularly those that are similar to the one you are proposing this time. If this is your first program, you're going to have to make even more of the credentials of the team you will have working with you. Include brief details about your camera operator, your editor and any other creative or technical personnel who will be making a contribution to the production. It may also be worth mentioning particular facilities that you plan to use and their reputation and track record.

Budget

This is best left till last. If the client has been delighted and impressed by everything they have seen so far, there is more of a chance they will accept what it is all going to cost. The next chapter goes into the detail of how you draw up a budget.

Presenting the Treatment

Wherever possible it is best to sell your ideas in person face to face with your client.

Broadcast

Researching the market

If you are trying to sell an idea to a broadcast organisation, research your market first. Check out their schedules and see if what you are proposing fits in to their program mix. Just because they already have three gardening programs does not necessarily mean they don't want another. It probably means gardening programs are very successful on their channel and their audience can't get enough of them. What you have got to come up with is a gardening program that is different.

Making contact

Once you have done that you need to find out who commissions the type of program you want to make. Try and talk to them by telephone. Give them an idea of what you have in mind. If the response is positive, try and arrange to go in and see them to present your treatment. If that fails, ask them if they would like you to send it in. There is still a chance that they will read it and ask you to come in and discuss it further.

Going via a production company

You may not want to go through all these hoops yourself. If you are primarily a program maker and not a salesperson, it might be best to take your ideas to an independent production company which already has strong contacts with the broadcasters. There is an element of risk in this approach. You will need to make an assessment of whether your chosen production company is trustworthy and will not walk off with your ideas and get someone else to execute them.

Corporate

Beauty parades

The approach for corporate videos will be different but the basic principles are the same. Always try and present your ideas in person to the individual who is going to commission the program. Corporate programs are often commissioned as a result of a **beauty parade**. A client may ask three or four producers to prepare treatments and costings for a particular program. Sometimes they will specify the budget limit. At other times they will specify the brief, ask for ideas and invite you to tell them what it will cost.

Preliminary meeting

Ask for a meeting with the client before you start putting your proposals together. This achieves two things. It shows you are taking the project seriously. It can also tell you how seriously the client is taking it. If the client says they are too busy, there is a fair chance they do not really intend to make a program but are just going through the motions of getting quotes to satisfy someone further up the organisation. Or it may be that they have already decided who is going to make the program and you are just on the list of producers to make up the numbers. The worst situation is where you won't just not get the job but the client will take your ideas and get someone else to produce them. It happens.

Assuming the client is serious about the program – and is seriously considering hiring you to make it – a preliminary meeting achieves several things. If the client doesn't know you already, the meeting is a chance for you both to get acquainted. If the client likes you personally and rates you as a professional you are nine-tenths of the way there. The client needs to feel you are a person they can get on with and work with.

A preliminary meeting also gives you the chance to probe the client's thinking and to get a first reaction to your ideas. There is nothing worse than producing what you think is a brilliant treatment and then finding out afterwards that it was rejected because the client had tried something similar before and it had been a dismal failure. Your client may also be asking you to do something that is going to be unrealistically expensive to produce. The preliminary meeting can be an opportunity to steer them towards doing something that will both work in communication terms and which will be within their budget.

Presentation

Once you have written the treatment you may be asked to present it in person or simply just to send it in. Either way, make it look as professional as possible. Don't just staple the sheets or send them off held together with a paper clip. A comb-bound document with a clear plastic cover and a card backing looks a lot better.

If you are not asked to present it in person, it is always worth asking if you can. Your competitors will probably be doing just that. If everybody is asking, the client may change their mind and get everyone in.

If you are definitely going to be presenting the treatment in person, there are a number of things you need to be thinking about. You may want to show them examples of other work you have done. So make sure there is a VCR and monitor available – and make sure you know how to work it. Find out how many copies of the presentation will be needed. As a general rule it is best to read out or deliver your presentation and then distribute copies of the document. Suggest at the outset that you make your presentation first and then take questions. If they have the document in front of them while you are speaking and are interrupting you with questions, you can lose your flow and they will lose their focus.

Be prepared for the questions the client may have. They may want to know how you are going to shoot particular sequences. They may want to test just how well you have thought through the ideas. They may want to query your costings. In many cases the client will not know a lot about the production process. So be ready to explain it simply with a minimum of technical jargon.

Start and end your presentation by thanking the client for the opportunity of making it.

CHAPTER 4
DRAWING UP A BUDGET

As we saw in the previous chapter you are going to have to work out at an early stage what your program is going to cost to produce. You may have been given a fixed budget to work from; you may have only a rough idea of what is available; or you may have been told – this is what we want to do, tell us what it will cost.

Whatever the situation, there are two key cost elements that will determine your budget. These are:

- the number of shoot days

- the total editing time you think you will need.

Almost everything else will flow from those two elements.

Estimating Shoot Days

If the program is to be shot mainly on location the number of shoot days will depend on the number of locations to be covered, their distance from one another, the number of set-ups per location and the time you think you will need for each set-up. If you are going to be shooting mainly in the studio you will need to estimate the number of studio days.

Estimating Editing Time

The amount of editing time you will require will depend to some extent on the final length of the program. As a rough guide, you should be able to offline edit anywhere between 6 and 10 minutes of finished program a day. But it is only a very rough guide. A 30 second sequence cut to music might take at least two hours to assemble, while a 30 second continuous soundbite might take only two minutes to view, select and edit into the program. So the amount of editing time you need will depend on the complexity of the program. It will also depend on how well prepared you are when you come to the edit. Online editing is a little easier to estimate. It is governed by two main factors: the program length and the complexity of the visual effects you want to include.

Getting Quotes

If this is your first production and you don't have access to your own or in-house facilities, you are going to have to spend some time on the telephone getting quotes. Most facilities will quote over the telephone but it is always best to get them to send you their rate card. That way you get to see what is included and what is not included. One camera crew might be cheaper than another but they may not include a wide angle lens as part of their standard package. On the other hand that crew might include some tracking equipment as standard while the other does not. You might decide you are going to dry-hire your offline edit suite and do the editing yourself. If there is not a lot of difference between the dry-hire rate and their rate with editor, you could reasonably suppose that they are overcharging for dry-hire. When you are getting quotes for online editing you may find that one facility includes a channel of special effects as standard while another charges it as an extra.

Calculating Costs

For the purposes of budgeting you can use the rates you are quoted to work out what your final costs are likely to be. Make a list:

•	Camera crew and equipment	£1000 per day
•	Offline editing	£500 per day
•	Online editing	£150 per hour

These are your **unit costs**.

Please note:
The figures above and all the figures we shall be using in the course of this chapter are for the purposes of illustration only.

The Basic Spreadsheet

Now you can multiply those unit costs by the number of hours or days you think you are going to need each of them. If you have a computer, use a spreadsheet to do this. If all you have is pen and paper the principle will be the same. The first five columns of a spreadsheet might look like this:

	A	B	C	D	E
1	Working Title:	LONDON TOUR			
2	Client:	BTA			
3	Production No:	9803			
4					
5					
6					
7	ITEM	NO of	DAYS/HRS	UNIT COST	COST
8					
9	CAMERA CREW	3	DAYS	1000.00	3000.00
10	OFFLINE EDIT	2	DAYS	500.00	1000.00
11	ONLINE EDIT	8	HOURS	150.00	1200.00
12	TAXIS	1		100.00	100.00
13					
14					
15					
16	SUBTOTAL				5300.00
17	INSURANCE				53.00
18					
19	TOTAL				5353.00

At the top of the spreadsheet we have given the production a working title, we show who it is being made for and show a production number. It is vital to give each production a working title and to use that title throughout. A production number is optional but it may be useful. Make sure the working title and production number are on all paperwork and all tapes. Our working title is 'London Tour' but in fact the program ends up being called 'Capital City'. It is best to stick with the working title throughout to avoid confusion.

Column A contains a brief description of each budget ITEM. In

Column B you enter the number of hours or days of a budget item you may need and in Column C you enter whether these are hours, days or whatever. In Column D you enter the unit cost per hour or day for each budget item. Column E contains a calculation: the cell contents of Column B times those of Column D – in other words the number of hours or days multiplied by the unit cost. You will see that the TAXIS item doesn't show any hours or days. In this example we have simply made an allowance of an overall figure for the production.

Now in Row 16 you can show the SUBTOTAL of all your costs with a calculated cell E16 which adds up the values in the range E9 through to E12.

Below the SUBTOTAL is INSURANCE. This is calculated in the example as a percentage of the bought-in costs, the SUBTOTAL. It is always advisable to insure your production, for example against loss of, or damage, to tapes. You should also be insured for any claims by hired personnel or members of the public. In the example we have assumed that insurance is being charged at 1% of the costs so the cell formula is E16*.01. If you add more budget items or change any of the figures in columns B or D the insurance will change automatically as will the TOTAL in Row 16 because this is also a formula – E16+E17, the SUBTOTAL plus the INSURANCE.

You now know your costs – the amounts you estimate you are going to have to pay out. In the example we have only shown four sample budget items. In reality you are likely to have considerably more than these. There's a checklist of some fairly standard budget items at the end of the chapter which you could incorporate into a template to save keying them in time and again.

Calculating Profit

If your program is being commissioned by either a broadcast or a corporate client, you now need to add another column in the spreadsheet. What the program costs you to make will not be what you charge your client. You need to be making a profit.

The standard way of calculating profit is to mark up your costs by a fixed percentage. In this example we are going to mark up the costs by 30%. So the spreadsheet will now look like this:

	A	B	C	D	E	F
1	Working Title:	LONDON TOUR				
2	Client:	BTA				
3	Production No:	9803				
4						
5						
6						
7	ITEM	NO of	DAYS/HRS	UNIT COST	COST	PRICE
8						
9	CAMERA CREW	3	DAYS	1000.00	3000.00	3900.00
10	OFFLINE EDIT	2	DAYS	500.00	1000.00	1300.00
11	ONLINE EDIT	8	HOURS	150.00	1200.00	1560.00
12	TAXIS	1		100.00	100.00	130.00
13						
14						
15						
16	SUBTOTAL				5300.00	6890.00
17	INSURANCE				53.00	68.90
18						
19	TOTAL				5353.00	6958.90
20						
21					EST	
22	PROFIT				1605.90	
23	MARGIN				23.08%	

We have added an additional column, F, and called it PRICE as it is the price you will be charging for the work. Each of the cells in Column F is calculated. The formula in this instance is each of the values in rows 9 to 12 of column E multiplied by 1.3. The subtotal for PRICE is the sum of those values and insurance has been marked up separately. The total price (Cell F19) is the sum of F16 and F17. The reason for doing it this way – rather than simply marking up your cost subtotal – is that you may need to vary the mark-up on individual items. If you are doing that you might want to insert an additional column which shows the actual mark-up for each item and use it to calculate the price.

Calculating Margin

You will see too that we have also added Rows 22 and 23 to show PROFIT and MARGIN. The profit figure is the price subtotal less the cost subtotal or F19–E19. The margin is calculated by dividing the profit subtotal by the price subtotal and expressing it as a percentage. You may have a target to reach which will almost certainly be expressed as the margin. By adjusting other figures or negotiating special rates you will know whether you are likely to hit that target.

Actual Costs and Profit

So far we have looked at the budget you draw up before a production. Once you have completed the production you will want to know what you have actually spent and what your final actual profit and margin are. So the final spreadsheet might look like this.

	A	B	C	D	E	F	G
1	Working Title:	LONDON TOUR					
2	Client:	BTA					
3	Production No:	9803					
4							
5							
6							
7	ITEM	NO of	DAYS/HRS	UNIT COST	COST	PRICE	ACTUAL COST
8							
9	CAMERA CREW	3	DAYS	1000.00	3000.00	3900.00	2800.00
10	OFFLINE EDIT	2	DAYS	500.00	1000.00	1300.00	550.00
11	ONLINE EDIT	8	HOURS	150.00	1200.00	1560.00	1050.00
12	TAXIS	1		100.00	100.00	130.00	98.00
13							
14							
15							
16	SUBTOTAL				5300.00	6890.00	4498.00
17	INSURANCE				53.00	68.90	53.00
18							
19	TOTAL				5353.00	6958.90	4551.00
20							
21					EST		ACTUAL
22	PROFIT				1605.90		2430.90
23	MARGIN				23.08%		34.60%

An extra column, G, has been added in which you enter the actual amounts spent against each budget item. As you can see camera crew costs were in fact £2800 rather than the £3000 you had estimated and so on. Cells 16 to 23 in Column G are all calculated cells which give you a final result which in this case happens to be in your favour. It doesn't always work like that.

Summing Up

At this point experienced spreadsheet users are probably saying to themselves, 'That's not how I would do it.' Great, if you can see a better way to do it, go to it and prosper. You will still have to follow the same principles and these are:

- Get accurate quotes for every budget item.

- Check what is included and what is not included from your suppliers.

- Make as accurate a forecast as you can of the number of days and hours you will need for each budget item.

- Keep a close check on what you are spending.

- If you are not getting what you expect, make a fuss at the time rather than waiting until the invoice arrives.

- Try and do deals. Camera crews will often work for a lower weekly rate than their daily rate multiplied by 5. An editing facility may well give you a special rate if you are editing a whole series of programs with them.

Budget Nasties

By and large most suppliers in the television business are reasonably honest, though like any industry it has its dishonourable exceptions. However, suppliers won't do your cost control for you. They want you to spend as much with them as possible.

DRAWING UP A BUDGET

Here are a few of the things that can happen if you are not careful:

- You work through a lunch break, having asked your camera crew whether they mind. They say 'No problem' and when you get their bill they have included a charge for NLB (no lunch break). They are within their rights.

- Your camera crew work a 10-hour day before charging overtime but you don't start until 11am and finish at 9pm. You are charged 3 hours overtime. The 10-hour day assumes 'normal' working hours. This doesn't always happen but you should have checked.

- Another camera crew works a 'normal' 10-hour day on location but also charges travel time from their base.

- You ask your camera crew to supply tape stock. Surprise, surprise they charge more than you would pay if you went to a tape stockist. Pay up.

- You are in an online edit for which you are paying by the hour. You stand the editor down for an hour while you have lunch. You are charged the full rate for that hour. This is a grey area. Check what the deal is first.

- You record a voice-over in a sound studio and they tell you beforehand that the rate is £100 per hour. What they don't tell you, unless you ask, is that you will be charged for tape stock and long-term storage on their system.

- All suppliers in the UK and the European Union quote prices ex-VAT. You will have to pay their price plus VAT and you may not be able to claim the VAT back unless you are registered for VAT yourself. This can hurt.

Standard Budget Items

Executive producer
Producer
Director
Script
Production manager
Production assistant
Camera crew and equipment
Lighting electrician
Lights
Grip
Tracking equipment
Tape stock
Studio
Presenter
Narrator
Actor
Costume
Make up artist
Rostrum camera
Graphics
Offline edit
Online edit
Sound record/dub
Mileage
Vehicle hire
Rail fares
Air fares
Meals
Accommodation
Taxis
Messengers

This list is by no means exhaustive and you may well need to break some of the items down even further. For example, you might have a 2-person crew for 3 days and a camera operator on their own for 2. In which case you would probably want to treat each as separate items.

Chapter 5
Writing a Script

There are two key points to remember about scripting:

* A television script is not just a commentary or dialogue. Your audience is going to be seeing pictures while they listen to the commentary. They will probably also be hearing incidental music and sound effects. A good script marries all of those elements so that they are working together.

* Any commentary is going to be spoken out loud. You must write commentary in such a way that it is easy for a narrator to read and easy for your audience to listen to and understand. The audience will only get one chance to hear it and they won't be able to see it. That may seem obvious but it means writing scripts is very different from writing something that is going to appear in print.

Technique

A scriptwriter is both a visualiser and a wordsmith. You need to be thinking pictures at the same time as you are thinking words.

You also need to be thinking about the flow, the structure and the pace of the overall program.

Because you are writing spoken words your style can afford to be less formal and more conversational than it might be if you were writing for the printed page.

You need to be as economical as possible with the number of words that you use. Television time is precious; not just in money terms but in terms of the audience's attention span. As a general rule commentary is delivered at the rate of two words per second. So in a minute of television you can deliver 120 words. It is not a lot of words but it is quite a long screen time.

A **golden rule** of scriptwriting is to use as few words as possible and to keep them as simple as possible. What you write may not look that impressive on paper. Don't worry. No-one is going to see what you have written.

The test is to read the words out loud and to ask yourself

*   was that easy to read?

*   was it clear?

*   will people get it first time?

Script Layout

Most scripts are laid out on the page in two parallel columns. In the left-hand column you describe what the audience will **see** and in the right hand column you describe what the audience will **hear** – the voice-over commentary, content of interviews, music and sound effects. By laying the script out this way you can immediately see how the sound and the pictures are going to work with one another. You are also starting to create the structure of the program.

For a program item shot on location your script might look like this:

SEE	*HEAR*
I Montage of London landmarks	MUSIC [Traditional 'London' theme]
2 Super Caption: CAPITAL CITY	
3 Pull back from Eros to reveal Presenter at Piccadilly Circus	Fade MUSIC PRESENTER sync: Welcome to London. In this program we'll be taking you on a

SEE	HEAR
	tour of Britain's capital city. And our guide for the day will be
4 Cut to black cab drawing up	the driver of one of London's famous black cabs
5 Close up Fred at wheel of cab	His name's Fred Smith
6 Cut to Presenter now in back of cab	Like all London cabbies, Fred knows this city like the back of his hand. Fred, how do you get to know a city the size of London?
7 Fred at wheel	FRED interview explaining how trainee cabbies have to spend
8 Cutaways of trainee cabby on motor bike and street signs	weeks riding round London on a motor bike learning street names and locations.
9 High angle shot of Fred's black cab	PRESENTER VO: And I soon found out that Fred's knowledge isn't confined to street names.
10 Fast montage of tracking shots of St Paul's, Buckingham Palace, Houses of Parliament	He knows all the sights . . . MUSIC [Elgar?]
11 Montage of top hotels	. . . all the top hotels

Numbering Shots

As you can from this example, the script is broken down by consecutive numbers. Each of these describes a separate shot or shots. This is essential when it come to planning the shoot. It gives the director a checklist of what has to be shot and what the accompanying sound will be. For example, Shot 8 is visuals of trainee cab drivers and street signs. In the finished program these will be pasted over 7, the interview with Fred. The script for a program shot in the studio will look slightly different and the process is described in Chapter 12. However, the basic principles and much of the terminology are the same.

Technical Terms

You may also have noticed terms such as **sync** and **VO**. Sync is an abbreviation for synchronous – two things that are both happening at the same time. In television this means that sound and picture are synchronous or in sync. The presenter will be shot speaking to camera and this what we will both see and hear. Any sync shot is a shot where, in the edited program, the original sound and picture run together exactly as they were recorded. Fred's interview will be shot sync but once you cut away to shots of trainees his sound becomes **non-sync**. Non-sync sound is also referred to as a **wildtrack**.

VO stands for voice-over. The voice-over commentary will be recorded separately as a wildtrack and then pictures will be matched up to it. For example, on Shot 9 what we are seeing is a high angle shot of the cab. The commentary will be voice-over, so it is shown as PRESENTER VO. If the program does not have an in-vision presenter and all of the commentary will be voiced over we would use the expression **MVO** (Male voice-over) or **FVO** (Female voice-over). If you decided to use a number of different voices, they might be identified as MVO1, MVO2, FVO1, FVO2, etc. Alternatively, you might use the names of characters (e.g. FRED VO) or the names of the actual voice-over artists but at this stage you may not have decided who they are going to be.

The other two principal elements on the *HEAR* side of the script will be music and sound effects. Sound effects are abbreviated as **SFX**. As you can see, the script also indicates where there will be music and suggests the type of music track that might be appropriate.

Showing Sequences

At first sight it is not that easy to read a script and to take in both what you are going to see and what you are going to hear. It is a matter of practice. You can make it easier both for yourself and for anyone who is going to be using the script by starting each sequence with a brief description of what is about to happen before you get into the detail. Breaking the script down by sequences gives you a good sense of how the overall program is going to be structured. On a drama script your sequence descriptions might include notes on how people are going to be dressed, how they sound, the characters they are playing and the settings for the action.

The description of the sequence should run right across the page and could be set in italics to show that it is not part of the script proper. You may well find that your treatment serves as a good framework for the structure and description of your sequences.

So our example above might have the following sequence descriptions:

Sequence 1:
Program opens with a 20" sequence of shots of well-known London landmarks cut to a traditional London theme

1   Montage of   MUSIC [Traditional 'London' theme]
     London
     landmarks

2   Super Caption:
     CAPITAL CITY

Sequence 2:
Female presenter in smart casual dress is first seen in Piccadilly Circus introducing us to our guide, a London cab driver called Fred. As they drive off in the cab, Fred explains how London cab drivers have to know the city inside out and then proceeds to take us on a tour.

3	Pull back from Eros to reveal presenter at Piccadilly Circus	Fade MUSIC
		PRESENTER sync:
		Welcome to London. In this program we'll be taking you on a tour of Britain's capital city. And our guide for the day will be
4	Cut to black cab drawing up	the driver of one of London's famous black cabs
5	Close up Fred at wheel of cab	His name's Fred Smith ... (etc.)

Words or Pictures First?

It is a question of personal choice whether you write the commentary first and then go back and add the pictures. The best way is to do both at the same time. That way you are getting a proper feel of how each sequence is going to work and how all the elements that make up the sequence are going to work together. If you go back and add pictures after you have written the voice-over, you run the risk of creating a boring commentary-led program. It could end up as radio with pictures rather than television.

As you write commentary keep on asking yourself:

Will there be enough good relevant pictures to work with these words?

If not, cut down on the words.

What Wordprocessor?

You will probably be writing your script on a PC or Mac. Most word processing applications allow you to format a document so that it looks like the script example. However, very few that this writer has ever come across really allow you to write straight to the page with parallel columns and numbering and, most important, then allow you to make changes easily. The one exception is WordPerfect.

 Tips

- Words and pictures should always be working together. Commentary does not need to describe what the viewer is seeing but it must relate to the pictures. If the pictures are strong enough you may not need any commentary at all. You can let the pictures speak for themselves.

- Avoid adjectives in commentary. You don't need to say that baby seals are 'furry and loveable'. The pictures should already be doing that.

- Keep commentary conversational. Use everyday language, the way people speak normally. For example, use 'But' rather than 'However'.

- You can break a lot of rules you learned in English lessons. You don't have to have a verb in every sentence. In fact it can be a lot more effective to say 'Fast, reliable, convenient – the Channel Tunnel' rather than 'The Channel Tunnel is fast, reliable and convenient'. Try reading them both out loud and decide which of the two you think is punchier. Then think about the first of the two and imagine how you would tie pictures to it. 'Fast' – a train streaks past the camera; 'reliable' – the driver in his high tech cab; 'convenient' – a passenger sitting back enjoying a drink; 'the Channel Tunnel' – cut out to wide shot of train entering the tunnel. The words and pictures are working together. The alternative line is simply a bald statement of fact and doesn't give you the same opportunity to create a visual impact.

- You may not need any commentary at all. You can often tell the story by assembling soundbites from interviews to create the narrative. But a certain amount of planning and careful shooting is needed to achieve this. Adopting this technique means you must be thinking all the time whether the interviews you are shooting will in fact cut together to create a narrative on their own.

- Keep it simple. Keep it short. Check facts. Check figures.

CHAPTER 6
PRE-PRODUCTION

There are two ways of putting a program together.

- One way is to leap out with a camera and start shooting. This is the fun way and you may get away with it. But the chances are that it will be a disaster and even if it isn't, you could have wasted a good deal of time, money and other people's goodwill.

- The other way is to prepare as thoroughly as you can. There are a hundred and one things you may need to do in pre-production and you're unlikely to have done them all before you start to shoot. Pre-production tasks have a habit of dragging on into the later stages as well.

First there's going to be a bit of paperwork. You will need to draw up a production schedule. If your program is being made to a deadline it is best to work back from the delivery date to work out when you are going to be doing what.

Schedules

If we take a simple example of a 10-minute program that has to be delivered within a month, the schedule might look something like this:

Week 1   Scripting
           Recces

Week 2   Shoot
           Graphics

Week 3   Offline edit

Week 4   Record commentary
           Online edit
           Sound dub
           Duplication

On the face of it this looks like quite a relaxed schedule but in fact it does not give much time in Week 1 for scripting and recces. Scripts seldom hit the mark first time and you could well be going out looking at locations while the scriptwriter is working on a second or third draft. Meanwhile, you find that one of the people you wanted to interview isn't available during Week 2 so you are going to have to juggle the schedule. You might find you have to do one day's shooting during Week 3 while you are editing. If you are making a corporate video your client will probably want to be approving script, offline edit and graphics at various stages. You will need to build those approval stages into the schedule and make sure the client is aware of them and has allowed time in their own schedule.

As a general rule it is always best for a schedule to be continuous and not to include long breaks between or within the stages. Sometimes this is out of your control and you may be obliged to shelve a project for a while and then return to it at a later date. This is not an ideal way of working but it is one that you may have to accept. This is all the more reason for being well organised and keeping careful records of what you have done and what you plan to do.

Blocking the Script

It is unlikely that you will be able to draw up a detailed schedule on your first day of pre-production. There is a lot you don't know yet about the production itself and things will keep changing. Once your script is written you can start **blocking** it to work out what you need to shoot. The word blocking comes from the theatre where it means working out all the moves. In television it means working out what you have to shoot and where and when you are going to do it. The simplest way to do this is to go through the script and make a note of the separate locations you will be shooting in. Once you have done that, go back over the script and write down beside each location what you have to shoot in each of them, using sequence and shot numbers as a reference.

We'll use the sample script from the previous chapter and imagine we now have a full script which ends with two shots of the presenter – Shots 50 and 51.The first part of the list could look like this:

City	Location	Shot	Shot No.
London	Piccadilly Circus	Presenter intro	3
		Cab drawing up	4
		Presenter getting in cab at start	6
		High angle shots of cab	9
		Presenter getting out of cab at end	50
		Presenter pay-off	51

This is the list of shots for a particular location in the order they appear in the script but it is not the order you are likely to shoot them in. The script calls for the presenter to deliver an intro and a pay-off to close the program. The camera position will be the same for both. So it makes sense to shoot them both at the same time. You don't want the cab in shot for the intro but you do want it in shot for the getting in, getting out and pay-off shots. So for Piccadilly Circus the order in which you shoot could change to look like this:

City	Location	Shot	Shot No.
London	Piccadilly Circus	Presenter intro	3
		Cab drawing up	4
		Presenter pay-off	51
		Presenter getting into cab at start	6
		Presenter getting out of cab at end	50
		High angle shots of cab	9

Estimating Shoot Time

Now you need to make an estimate of how long it is going to take you to shoot and what time of day will be best. The first thing to remember about this location is that there is nowhere to park. The best plan might be to park your camera vehicle in a nearby car park and carry the gear to Piccadilly Circus. That little operation might take you half an hour. Assuming a 9.00am start you will probably not be ready to shoot until 9.45am. How long will it take to shoot the presenter's intro and pay-off? They are only 15 seconds each and she doesn't need a prompt system. Allowing for retakes, it shouldn't take more than 15 minutes but you should let the presenter have the script before the shoot and say you are expecting it to be learned in advance.

The schedule is starting to take shape. You should be ready to shoot the presenter getting in and out of the cab by about 10.00am. Again, with a bit of luck, that might take you another 15 minutes. You can schedule the high angle shots of the cab for 10.30am – allowing for the time it is going to take you to strike the gear and take it up five floors in a lift to the top-floor office you have arranged to shoot from. You can expect to be out of the building again by about 11.00am when you will start shooting the interview with Fred in his cab. You expect that will take the rest of the morning.

So now your schedule is looking like this:

		Shot No.
0900	RV park in NCP car park Poland St	
	Carry camera equipment to Piccadilly Circus	
0945	Shoot Presenter intro	3
	Cab drawing up	4
	Presenter pay-off	51
1000	Presenter getting into cab at start	6
	Presenter getting out of cab at end	50
1030	High angle shots of cab	9
1100	Shoot interview in cab	7
1300	LUNCH	

It is always a good idea to show meal breaks in your schedule. They may not actually happen on time or even happen at all but they make everyone feel happier.

This is just a small part of the full shooting schedule you will be drawing up. As well as giving timings it also needs to list names and telephone numbers of everyone on the production and everyone you will be dealing with. This is also known as the **call sheet**. In particular it should make clear where everyone should meet up – the **RV** or rendezvous point. Make location addresses as detailed as possible. Postal addresses don't always give the full story. Include directions on how to reach the location but even better is a map. Directions you may have been given down the phone may not be that accurate. With a map there is less chance of a mistake.

So far this schedule tells everyone on the team about the timings but there are a few other details to attend to.

Permissions

If you are shooting in a major city you may need to inform the police well in advance. Normally, they won't be too bothered by a small unit of two or three people but they can get difficult, particularly if you are blocking public thoroughfares. In the example we have been looking at, you are not going to be able to walk in off the street and get the high angle shots you want. You will need to have cleared it with the building's owners or tenants first and they may want a facility fee. Don't assume that the person who has agreed to let you use their office for shooting will have told their own security people.

Be prepared for the receptionist or security officer to know nothing about the fact that you are coming that day. In a perfect world it is best to have talked to them yourself beforehand so that this minor change to their routine doesn't come as a total shock. If you are not able to do that, make sure when you come to shoot you have with you the name of the person who has given you permission and, ideally, a letter from them confirming the arrangements.

The Sun

In the example above you will probably have chosen the building you want to shoot from as a result of a location recce some time before the shooting. Try and recce a location at the same time of day as you hope or expect to be shooting it. You will need to know what the sun is likely to be doing. If it isn't shining when you recce or it is a different time of day from your planned shoot time, take a compass with you and check what might be happening. Just in case you've forgotten your basic geography, the sun rises in the east, moves south rising all the time, reaches the south at midday and then travels west gradually dipping until it disappears. It never shines from the north.

So to get your high angle shot your best bet will be to choose a building facing south. The light source will be directly behind the camera evenly lighting the area you will be shooting. At 11.00am it will also be close to its highest point so there is less risk of its causing the building itself to throw shadows onto the street.

Interiors

You will also need to think about what the sun will be doing if you are shooting interiors. You will have problems if the natural daylight is streaming in through the windows while you are trying to use artificial light to shoot by. They won't mix. If you want to shoot with the windows and exterior view in the background you will probably only be able to do so if the windows face north or east. Otherwise, make sure the windows have blinds or curtains or shoot looking away from them.

In many cases with modern cameras you may not need to worry about bringing in your own lights. In most well-lit factories and offices you can very often shoot general shots using the available light. But you won't get good results on close up shots or on interviews. If you need to bring in lights make sure there is an adequate power supply available. You will in any case probably want to run your camera off the mains whenever you can to save on batteries. If in doubt, consult an electrician.

If you are going to be shooting interviews try and get to see the room or office that is available before you shoot. In someone else's work environment you won't always be able to use their actual office. You may be offered a meeting room or a spare office. Try and choose somewhere as spacious as possible. You need room to work and you will get better results if you are able to light it properly and get some distance between the camera and the subject.

Estimating Shots

In a perfect world a location is recced by the director, lighting director, camera operator and production manager. They then treat themselves to a long lunch, five minutes of which is spent discussing the forthcoming shoot and the remainder swapping gossip. In the real world probably only the director or the production manager will get to recce a location.

One of the things a director will want to know from a recce is whether the camera is going to be able to frame the shots that are wanted. With a bit of experience you can do this by eye. You can also buy an expensive viewfinder and walk round looking through it to see things as the camera will – so long as you don't mind people thinking you are a bit of a poseur. Alternatively, there is a DIY viewfinder called your two hands. Make a frame with the right hand turned in and the left hand turned away from you and the thumb and forefinger of both sticking out at right angles.

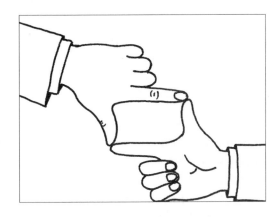

Look through the frame with one eye closed and push it away or towards you. It's a good guide to what the camera will see.

The advanced version is this: but you will only need it if you are shooting on 35mm film or for wide screen format.

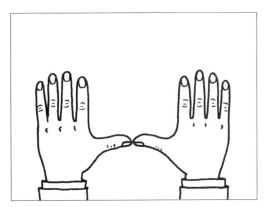

You may also want to see what the effect of a zoom lens would be if you were in tight on details of an exterior. The view through a pair of binoculars will give you a fair idea.

Transport

If you are moving between different locations you are going to need some form of transport. Most hired crews come with their own transport, normally a small van or people carrier. If you are doing your own shooting you will need something similar. Try and keep the number of vehicles to a minimum. If everyone can travel together there is less likelihood of people getting lost and you will have fewer parking problems. Always try and arrange adequate parking in advance of the shoot. Once you are in a building you will find it a lot easier to move about if you can pile all your equipment onto a small trolley.

Food and Drink

Sorry to sound like your mother but try not to skip meals. You'll just end up tired and bad tempered and the job will suffer. If your schedule does force you to skip a meal, try and let everyone know well in advance so they can stock up with snacks, chocolate, cigarettes (unfortunately some people do still use them) or whatever else they know will keep them going. Try and arrange supplies of coffee, tea or soft drinks through the day. Check beforehand there will be places you can get fed when you are shooting on location. Everyone is burning up mental and physical energy on a shoot. It needs replacing.

Chapter 7
Location Shooting –
The Equipment

This chapter assumes that you won't actually be operating equipment yourself. So we will keep the technical detail to a minimum, enough for you to understand what is available, what it can do, what it can't do and what you need to be thinking about to make your operators' lives as straightforward as possible. We are going to assume that you are shooting on Beta SP.

Camera

If you have ever used a domestic camcorder, you will find that the basic controls on a professional video camera are not so very different. At the front of the lens is the **focus ring** and just behind it is the **zoom ring**. To focus on a particular object the operator zooms in as tight as possible on that object, focuses on it and then zooms out again to the desired framing. This ensures that the object will always be in focus whether zooming in or out from it in the course of a take.

The zoom on electronic cameras is controlled by a pressure sensitive rocker switch on the pan handle. The operator controls the speed of the zoom by varying the pressure applied to the switch. However, to achieve a crash zoom – going in or out very fast – the operator uses a bar attached to the zoom ring and operates the zoom manually.

In the viewfinder the operator of a standard Beta SP camera will only be seeing a monochrome (black and white) picture. To check the colours and lighting a small colour monitor showing the camera's output will also be needed. Electronic cameras are fairly 'smart' but they do need some information to work from. As you move from one set-up to another, light and colour conditions will be different. In each set-up it is vital to do a **white balance**. You show the camera a plain piece of white paper and it then adjusts to conditions in that set-up.

Cameras can be powered either by a rechargeable battery –
attached to the rear of the camera – or mains supply. Wherever
possible it is best to use the mains supply. There are few things
more annoying than having to change a battery just as an
interview is getting interesting.

Most cameras come with the recorder attached. Both sound and
picture are recorded onto cassettes, normally with a running time
of approximately 35 minutes. You can get Beta SP tapes with
longer running times but you then usually have to use a separate
record machine. You can always check how much tape you have
got left by looking at the time code counter on the side of the
camera. You also use the time code counter to read off the start
and end points of each shot or take.

Time Code

You use time code to measure and identify everything at every
stage of the shooting and editing process. Without proper time
codes your editing machines will have no reference to work from.
So a few words of explanation are necessary.

Tape is measured in minutes, seconds and frames. The standard
speed at which tape runs on the PAL system is 25 frames per
second. You also need to identify each of your tapes by number.
So time code is expressed as roll number:minute:second:frame.
Once you have loaded a new cassette, you set the roll number
manually and the recorder does the rest.

If you are 20 minutes, 4 seconds and 8 frames into Roll 3, your
time code will look like this 03:20:04:08. That is what will show on
the time code counter on the side of the camera. It is also being
recorded invisibly on the tape itself. There may be instances
where you want the time code to be showing the actual time of
day; for example where you are shooting an event continuously
from start to finish on several cameras. You can switch the
recorder to show time of day code.

Sound

Your camera will have its own microphone but you should never rely on the on-camera mike for anything other than the most basic background sound.

There are no absolute rules about what mike you should use for what shot. Individual sound recordists will have their own preferences, as will directors. Many news programs like their reporters to be seen holding a microphone emblazoned with the station's ident as they report from the thick of the action. Technically, this is quite unnecessary and most program makers do their utmost to keep mikes out of shot. Miniature **personal mikes** can be attached to a necktie, shirt-fly or lapel and are hardly noticeable. Very often a **gun** or **rifle mike** can be held just out of shot, either above or below the visible action. Or the mike can be on a **boom** or **fishpole**. This allows the recordist to keep well back from the action – and out of shot – and cover sound closely and accurately.

Personal mike

Whatever mikes you are using, every care should be taken to hide or disguise cables. If a presenter or interviewee is wearing a personal mike the cabling should be fed down inside their clothing so that it is not visible. Sound recordists seem to enjoy this part of their job. If the subject is to be shot moving about and you want to be sure of catching everything they are saying then **radio mikes** are probably the answer. There is no cable leading from the mike to the recorder but the subject will have to have a small transmitter attached to their person. This can be a dead giveaway on many a

Gun or rifle mike

Boom or fishpole

so-called fly-on-the-wall documentary. Look for the bulge in the back pocket. Added to which, radio mikes are not 100% reliable.

On Beta SP you have the option of recording onto two separate sound tracks. This can be useful if you are recording two voices on two separate mikes and want to have maximum flexibility when you edit. If you are recording more than two voices you can either try and cover them all with a boom mike or you can put them on separate mikes. With separate mikes you know they are all covered but you will need to use a mixer and fade up each mike as it used. Leaving all the faders open is not a sensible option. All of the mikes will be picking up ambient sound and the result will be poor quality sound. With a boom mike, mixing on site is not necessary but the boom operator must either know in advance or be quick to anticipate who is going to speak when.

When you are shooting on location, conditions for recording sound are never perfect. In modern offices you may want to try and get the air conditioning switched off. It may not be noticeable to your ears but it will be there on the soundtrack. Wherever you shoot it is always advisable to shoot a **buzz track** of the ambient sound. When you come to edit you can use this to smooth over what can otherwise be ugly edits in your soundtrack. If you are recording voice and there is a strong background sound – e.g. a factory or busy street – at least with a buzz track you can make the background sound appear to be consistent.

Always think about potential sound problems and how you are going to get round them when you recce a location. A large, empty room where the sound reverberates will not be good. If in doubt, stand in the middle of the room and clap your hands. If there is any hint of an echo you are going to have a problem.

Lighting

There are two reasons you may need special lighting when you shoot on location:

- to help the camera 'see'
- to create an aesthetic effect.

Electronic cameras do not need as much help to see as film cameras do, so very often you can shoot without special lights in well-lit interiors. But if you are shooting interviews indoors you will almost always need some lights. The standard kit carried by most camera crews will usually be enough for this. Most carry two **blondes** and three **redheads** or their equivalents. Blondes are 2000 watt lamps traditionally with yellow heads (or shells) used to light fairly large areas – also referred to as 2Ks – and redheads smaller 800 watt lamps traditionally with red shells to light faces. Without any lights you will often get a picture but it won't be a good picture. You often need to use light to 'lift' a face. Domestic lighting is usually overhead and designed solely to help the human eye. Once you put a camera on a face or an object it starts to see shadows which may partially obscure the object or which just don't look good.

The conventional lighting set-up for an interview is to use three lights – key, fill and back light. The key light illuminates the interviewee's face, the fill light is a softer light set the other side of the camera to lift shadows thrown by the key. The back light is placed out of shot behind the interviewee and has the

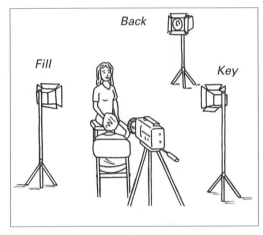

effect of separating the interviewee from the background.

If you then wanted to shoot a wide shot of the whole room in which the interview is taking place, you would probably strike (take out) the spot and fill lamps and use a blonde to light the foreground. There are no iron laws about this. Every situation is different and individual operators have their own ways of doing things. If a director is unsure about what lamps will be needed it is always best to recce locations beforehand with the lighting director or camera operator. This will add to your costs and the people needed may not be available on the days the director is able to recce. So if you are not a technician and you are doing a lighting recce on your own, these are a few things to watch for:

Checklist for lighting recces

☐ Is there an adequate power supply?

☐ Is there enough available artificial light to shoot without special lights? A simple test is to narrow your eyes as you look. It gives a rough approximation of what the camera will be able to see and register.

☐ Does the room have a lot of windows? If so, can you shoot what you want without the camera having to look at the windows? Natural daylight is a lot more intense than artificial light and can give you problems. Alternatively, are there blinds or curtains you can close to minimise the problem?

☐ Light backgrounds reflect light, dark backgrounds soak it up. If you are shooting against a background of dark wood panelling, you may need extra light. Similarly big, black lumps of machinery on a factory floor will look just like that unless you light them to show the detail.

☐ Will you need an electrician? The answer is probably 'yes' if you are going to need any more than the standard set of lights carried by your camera operator or if you have a number of set-ups to cover in a day. The extra pair of expert hands will save you a lot of time. You should definitely include an electrician in the crew if the power supply is questionable. If you overload someone's circuits and their computers all crash you will not be popular.

Achieving good lighting results takes care and time. Program makers are often under pressure to get material shot as quickly as they can and don't allow enough time or budget for lighting. They then wonder why their pictures don't look that good. Both director and camera operator should always take a long, hard look at the colour monitor to check for lighting problems before shooting.

Lighting Nasties

- the lighting is too 'hot'. Not only is it uncomfortable for the person being shot but their face is starting to shine. One solution is to soften the light by clamping a layer, or layers, of scrim to the barn doors – the hinged flaps around each lamp. It may also be necessary to apply some face powder to the person's face or, particularly, to a shiny bald pate.

- 'flares' and 'hot spots'. Always check that there is nothing in your picture that is picking up your light and reflecting it back at you. Glass and other shiny surfaces are the worst offenders.

- light stands or cables are in shot. The camera operator may not see them in the monochrome viewfinder.

Safety

You are going to be running live electrical cables across floors and walkways where people will not normally be expecting them. Always **tape them down** with gaffer tape so no one trips over them and brings light stands crashing down on their heads.

Exterior Lighting

Unless you are shooting a big budget drama you are unlikely to be using lights outdoors. However, in poor light conditions you may want to get some light on a person's face to lift the picture. You can either use a **sun gun**, a small hand-held lamp with its own battery, or a **reflector board**, a silvered piece of stretched cloth or board that is held to reflect what little sunlight there may be onto a person's face.

Always think about where the sun is going to be when you come to shoot. Plan your schedule around it for exteriors. If the sun is behind clouds see what the clouds are doing. If they are likely to clear and give you just five seconds of sunlight it is worth the wait. You will get a much better picture. On the other hand, if you are shooting an interview outdoors you may want the sun to be behind clouds all the time so that you have even light throughout.

Again, it is always worth waiting for the 'window'. Remember, too, that a grey sky can often give you bigger problems than a clear blue sky. On tape it will tend to burn out so you may need to frame shots to avoid seeing too much grey sky. You may want to use a **filter** to make an otherwise grey sky look blue.

Grip Equipment

There is a whole host of equipment you can hire to help you get visually interesting shots and various ways you can improvise to achieve similar effects. The hire companies will be only too happy to show you what they have got and what it will do. Broadly speaking this type of equipment breaks down into four categories – cranes, dollies, mounts and steadicam.

Cranes allow you to achieve high angle shots with the camera either rising up from, or descending, to ground level. The best type of crane is the **cherry picker** but it is expensive and usually only used on exteriors. A simpler type of crane is the **jib arm** which can be used in relatively confined spaces but which cranes up and down to greater heights than you would achieve on the tripod.

A **dolly** is a four wheeled platform on which the camera sits. The dolly itself runs along specially laid track. You can incorporate a dolly and a jib arm so that the camera can both travel and either elevate or depress at the same time.

Mounts are used to fix the camera onto a moving object such as a car, either to shoot from the car, to shoot a close up of its wheels or to shoot the car's occupants. Alternatively, you can shoot people in a car with a hand-held camera but it can get awkward for everybody. You won't get a very good shot and the camera is unlikely to remain steady.

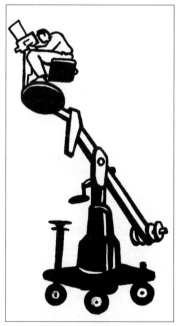

Jib arm and dolly

Steadicam is a harness system that the operator wears which allows the camera to effectively float in the air in front of him. It is ideal for shooting long sequences involving continuous movement. If properly operated it produces a rock steady picture without the need to lay track and use a dolly. In theory you can use steadicam to go upstairs, downstairs, along corridors, into and out of rooms.

Steadicam

The poor man's alternative to steadicam is to shoot **hand-held**. Some operators are better at this than others and the results will vary. Holding the camera dead steady and walking backwards at the same time is not easy. You may think it looks acceptable at the time but when you get to view your material in the edit suite, be prepared for disappointment.

If you cannot afford a dolly and track, you may get acceptable results by using the **rolling spyder**. This is a spreader on which the tripod sits with small wheels attached. Strictly speaking it is designed purely for moving the camera and tripod around from one set-up to another but on the right surface it can be used for tracking shots.

Rolling Spyder

Improvising Grip Equipment

You can also try mounting the camera and tripod on a trolley or lashing the camera to a supermarket trolley. But be warned. If you are not using specially laid track, the floor needs to be as smooth as possible and very few are. The slightest bump on the floor will show on your pictures. If you are shooting in a factory or workplace, you may be able to use a fork lift truck to good effect. Wheelchairs also make good mobile platforms and of course you can shoot through the open window of a moving car on a well-made road. You can also get good results with the operator standing up in a car with the sunroof open and shooting hand-held. One American cameraman the author worked with had a habit of opening the passenger door, standing on the sill, holding himself on with one hand and shooting with the other to achieve the same effect. This is not advised. He put on quite a show for the other drivers on the six-lane freeway but the pictures were rubbish.

Prompters

How do newsreaders and presenters manage to remember all their words? You know the answer. They don't. They use a tele-prompt system, usually referred to as autocue, though Autocue is in fact a proprietary name as in Hoover/vacuum cleaner. The autocue consists of a hood which fits on the front of the camera. The camera shoots through the hood. Meanwhile the presenter is looking at a screen on which

Autocue

the script is rolling up from bottom to top. It is quite literally all done with mirrors. The autocue operator sits at a box of tricks linked to the hood which allows them to control the speed at which the script is rolling. The operator can also adjust the size of the typeface. The operator will either have keyed in or imported from disk the text of the script and is able to make changes just as on an ordinary word processor.

Because the autocue hood is mounted directly in front of the lens, the presenter appears to be talking straight into the camera. You can also position the autocue just to one side of the camera. You may want to do this with a particularly inarticulate company Chairman on a corporate video to make it look as if he is giving you a spontaneous interview announcing a set of brilliant results. But it usually shows. A cheaper alternative with the same subject is to write out some key words on a flip chart and get him to talk to the flip chart as if it was an interviewer. He probably won't notice the difference.

Most professional presenters won't need any coaching on how to use autocue but you may be working with amateurs, corporates or reporters who are just taking their first leap into electronic stardom after a gruelling apprenticeship on their local papers. There are some pretty simple guidelines for them to follow:

☐ Focus your eyes on the centre of the screen. Don't swivel them from left to right and back again to follow the words. You don't need to.

☐ Deliver the script at your own pace. The autocue operator will slow down or speed up with you. The presenter is in control.

As far as production management is concerned, there are a number of points you need to remember if you are going to be shooting on location using autocue:

☐ Try and arrange parking and a trolley. The kit comes in four or five fairly hefty boxes.

☐ Warn your camera crew in advance. There may be a piece of kit they need to bring with them to make sure it marries up with the camera.

☐ Try and let autocue have your script in advance of the shoot as both hard copy and as a computer file. Check what format they can handle. Most systems are PC-based and will accept an ASCII text file or a file created in one of the more common word-processing programs.

☐ If you are sending a computer file, delete all your shot descriptions and anything else apart from the words that are actually going to be spoken.

One of the drawbacks of autocue is that it restricts camera movement and means that your presenter has to be close enough to the camera to read the screen. If that's a problem and you want the presenter to be seen in the distance or moving about, there's an alternative to autocue known as **the wire**. The presenter records the script onto a standard cassette, hides a small battery-powered cassette player about their person, to which is connected a small earpiece. The presenter then plays the words back into their own ear and speaks off them. Not all presenters can do this so don't insist on the method unless they are used to it. They're just going to have to learn the script and remember it. You're usually paying them enough.

Chapter 8
Location Shooting –
Techniques

This chapter is mainly about the terminology of shooting – the common language everybody uses to describe shots. It also offers suggestions as to the impact you can achieve by using one type of shot rather than another, what will work and what will not work. Most of the terms apply whether you are shooting on location or in a studio.

Types of Shot

The most basic shot is the **static**. The camera doesn't move and the size of shot remains constant. It sounds boring but the vast majority of shots you see on television are static shots. The key to making them interesting is the action – what is happening in the shot.

On a fixed tripod when you traverse the camera horizontally from left to right or right to left you are executing a **pan** or **panning shot**.

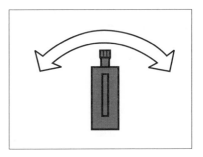

Pan

If the camera itself is moving in either direction you are executing a **track** or **tracking shot**.

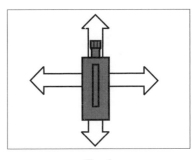

Track

Similar to a track is a **crab**. The camera moves crab-like in a slight arc, possibly panning slightly at the same time.

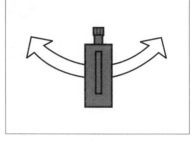

Crab

As a general rule it is always best to pan or track from left to right. That is the way our eyes are accustomed to work when we read. If you don't believe it, pick up a camera and try panning it both ways on a static subject such as a row of houses. You will find the pan from left to right feels more comfortable. The right to left pan can induce a slight queasiness unless you are panning with an object that is itself moving from right to left.

When the camera moves through the vertical axis on a fixed tripod, it is said to be **tilting up or down**. This is also referred to as a pan up or down.

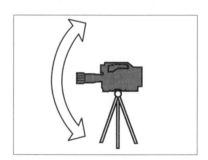

Tilting up or down

If you are using a crane or jib arm and the camera itself is moving up or down you would talk about it either **elevating** or **depressing** or **craning up and down**.

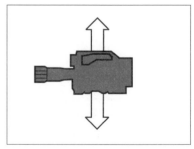

Elevating/depressing or craning up/down

Shot Sizes

There is a standard language used to describe shot sizes. These are expressed in terms of shooting a human figure. A **long shot** generally means a full-length shot. Cutting off at around the knees is a **medium long shot**, at the waist a **mid shot**, at the breast-pocket of a man's jacket a **medium close up**, just below the tie a **close up** and going in even tighter a **big close up**. These would be abbreviated on a script or log as LS, MLS, MS, MCU, CU and BCU.

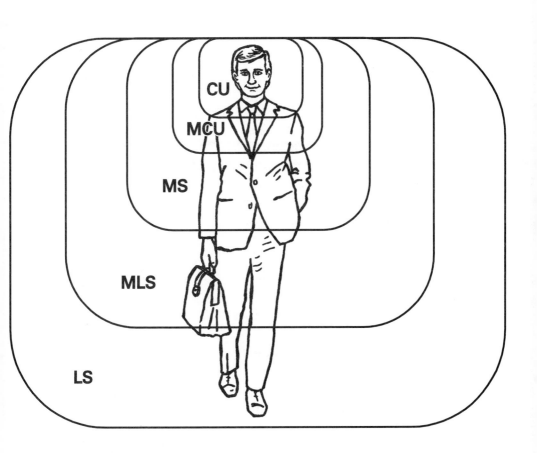

LOCATION SHOOTING – TECHNIQUES

These two pictures show the relative difference between close up and big close up.

CU

BCU

You can apply the terms as an easy reference to anything you are shooting, not just human figures. You might talk about a long shot of a house with a person in the foreground, followed by a mid shot of the house and a close up of the front door. The terms are really just a way of describing the relative sizes of shots of the same scene or subject and you need not get hung up on them.

Long shot

You may also want to describe shots in terms of the position of the camera relative to the subject – a **low angle** or **high angle** shot – LA and HA. Finally there is the **wide angle** or WA. Strictly speaking this is a reference to the lens angle but everyone uses it to describe a wide shot that shows all the action or a group of people.

Mid shot

Close up

Changing Shot Sizes

There are two ways of changing the size of your shot. You can either **zoom** in or out or you can **track** in or out. To track the camera you will need to be on a dolly of some sort and the lens will need to be set at a wide angle. Tracking with the camera zoomed tight on a narrow lens never works. You would need to be constantly adjusting the focus – a near impossibility – and the slightest movement of the camera will result in an extremely jerky and unstable picture.

There is quite a difference between the visual effect of a zoom in and a track in. When you zoom in you are actually changing the lens angle all the time. The background is continuously shrinking and defocusing. When you track in the lens angle remains constant. The viewer has a sense of actually moving in on the subject rather than simply seeing the subject get bigger in the screen. If you have an opportunity, try it both ways and you will see the difference.

There is a standard language used when changing or setting up shot sizes. If you want the camera to zoom in or out slowly and gently you would talk about **easing in** or **easing out**. If you want to adjust a shot to be a tiny little bit tighter you would talk about easing in or out a **gnat's** – as in gnat's whisker – i.e. something imperceptibly narrow.

Describing Shots

Another way of describing shots is to refer to the number of people appearing in them. A shot showing just one person is referred to as a **single**, one showing two people a **2-shot**, one with three people in it a **3-shot**. When you get past three people you would probably talk about a **group shot** or the wide angle.

In any shot with more than two people in it you are likely to be seeing more of one person's face than those of the others. You would therefore describe that shot as **favouring** that person.

The illustration shows a 2-shot of a female reporter with male interviewee favouring the interviewee. As we can see quite a lot of both of them, we would describe this as a **loose 2-shot**. This would probably be shot with the camera zoomed out on its widest angle so you might also call this a **wide angle 2-shot**.

Loose 2-shot favouring interviewee

Let's suppose you shoot a 2-shot looking the other way.

Now you are favouring the woman interviewer. This is referred to as the **reverse angle**. It also happens to be a much tighter shot showing far less of the two people so it is described as a **tight 2-shot**. To achieve it the operator has actually moved the camera further away from the subjects and then zoomed in tighter. The foreground figure would be slightly **soft** or out of focus while the interviewee is **sharp** or in focus.

Reverse angle tight 2-shot

Point of View

Most of the time the camera views things as a third party. In the 2-shots above the camera is an observer and is not part of the action. But let's say one of the people in the shot was looking down at something and you wanted to shoot the object as it would be seen by that person. You would call that a **pov** shot or point of view shot. We might see a man walking towards camera and then cut to a tracking shot with the camera simulating his walk as it moves towards a door. This would be shot from the man's point of view. The camera would have become part of the action.

· A Bit of Art

The further the camera is away from a subject or subjects and the narrower the lens angle, the more critical the focus will be. You can put this to good effect by **throwing** or **pulling focus** from one object to another.

You might have two people in a tight 2-shot, both facing the camera but with one a few feet behind the other.

Each time one of them speaks you pull focus to make their image sharp and that on the other person soft. You are more likely to do this on a drama than a news program. But there are numerous ways you can use the technique. Familiar examples include throwing focus from one flower to another or from a barbed wire fence to the starving prisoners behind it. Another favourite is to start completely defocused on a city night scene. When the camera is defocused all the viewer sees is an interesting little light show. As you focus up the image is revealed.

Chromakey

If you want to add a background to an interview talking head you can shoot the subject against a blue or green screen and then **key in** whatever picture you want in the online edit. The new background picture will fill any part of the original picture that contains either blue or green. So it is absolutely vital that the interviewee is not wearing anything containing the colour you

Person shot against chromakey screen

Background picture shot separately

Both pictures keyed together

have chosen as your chromakey colour. It is also important that your blue or green screen is evenly lit. The technique can be effective but if you are shooting on location with only one camera and standard equipment you do not have an absolute assurance that it is going to work. If your subject has fuzzy or thinning hair and you can see through their hair to the screen you will not get clean separation between foreground and background pictures.
Chromakey is also referred to as **CSO** or **colour separation overlay**.

A Few Rules

Innovation is the lifeblood of any industry and television is no exception. But the fact is that 99% of all shooting for television follows a number of rules. You need to know them before you work out ways of breaking them.

The guidelines for framing and composing shots for television are very similar to those for still photography but there are important differences.

Headroom: on a static shot of a talking head always allow sufficient headroom or clear space above a person's head (on a big close up this does not apply). But some of the headroom you see in the viewfinder will be lost in cutoff.

Cutoff: domestic television monitors will almost always cut off the edges of the picture you see in your viewfinder. The monitor you use for shooting should allow you to switch between what the camera can see and 'puntervision' – the 'safe' area that a domestic monitor is likely to show. You always need to compose shots to allow for any cutoff.

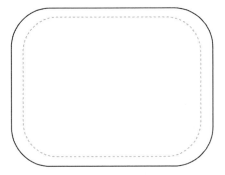

Domestic TV set may cut off area of picture outside dotted line

Shot framed for the camera without allowing for cutoff

On domestic monitor shot is tighter than you wanted with no headroom

Framing: on a static talking head where the person is looking camera right, the framing should place the person to the left of the picture rather than in the centre. Give the person some **looking space**. If you are panning with a person walking or a vehicle on the move, don't place them in the centre of the picture – allow them some **leading space** ahead of themselves.

Allowing looking space

Foreground: try and add a frame to your pictures by including something in the foreground. The shot of the house alone is boring. The shot of the house with tree and overhanging branch in foreground is a bit more interesting. The overhanging branch or similar is known in the trade as **dingle**.

Without dingle   *With dingle*

Pans: as a general rule pans should start and end with something. There should be a reason for panning. A pan that tells a story might start on a For Sale sign and pan to the house in question. The shot will be further improved if you have someone walk past the sign and then up to the house as you pan. You have introduced some action and given the camera a reason to pan.

Zooms: overuse of the zoom is a sure sign of an amateur at work. Think of the zoom as a means of changing from wide angle to close up quickly. A straight cut from the wide to the close is often far more effective than having to sit and watch the camera at work. Chop out the zooms in the edit wherever possible or only keep them in if they really are achieving a strong visual effect. Zooming out from a subject to reveal something unexpected can be effective but don't just zoom for the sake of it.

Take a look at some well made, popular TV programs. Count the number of times you see an in-vision zoom. Very seldom, except on the news where the camera operator is having to grab action.

Holds: it is always best to shoot a static hold at the beginning and end of any shot involving camera movement. It will make life far easier when you come to edit. Don't just switch on and start to pan or zoom immediately. Hold for a second or two and then start the camera movement. You can always lose the hold but you can't add it if you need it.

Rehearsal: wherever you can, try and rehearse any shot involving movement or action – even something as simple as our person walking past the For Sale sign and up to the house. Tape is not that cheap and you will save time in the edit if you are not having to search through all the duff takes.

Instructions

Once a shot has been set up the director should check that everybody is ready. If the camera operator is happy with the lighting the director says:

'Turn over'

At this point the sound recordist says 'Hang on, I haven't taken a level yet'.

The sound recordist gets the person being shot to say a few words and makes any necessary adjustments. This has probably happened because the director didn't warn the sound recordist they were about to start shooting. The director tries again.

'Turn over'

The camera operator starts to record, allows time for picture and time code to stabilise (usually up to 10 seconds) and says:

'Speed'

The director then says:

'Action'

With a bit of luck everything then starts to happen according to plan. Once the action is completed, the director says:

'Cut'

If the shot is not working out as planned, the director will probably call 'Cut' sooner to save tape and sort out the problem. On other occasions the director may want to continue shooting after the point at which the camera operator may think he should cut. In that case the director would say 'Keep running' or 'Keep rolling'.

At the end of a day's shooting the director will say **'That's a wrap for today'.** But before saying so, the director should make absolutely sure there is nothing else to shoot. People and equipment have a habit of disappearing very fast once those magic words are spoken.

Making It Happen

If you are directing for the first time, you need not worry too much about using exactly the right words. What is important is that you communicate as fully as possible with everyone on the team. They each need to know what you want to do and what you want to achieve. It is important to brief your sound recordist as fully as your camera operator. If you are planning a wide shot with full sound, the sound recordist needs to know so as to think about how to get the results you want without mikes or cables appearing in shot. A good camera operator will want to know how one shot is going to cut with another and will shoot them so that they do. So it is worth talking through how you see a sequence working with your shoot team. They will often make helpful suggestions and you can learn a lot from their experience.

Very few successful television programs are made without a high degree of teamwork between those involved. Part of the director's job is as an on-site people manager who makes sure people are fully informed and working well together.

Logging Shots

In a perfect world everything should be logged on paper as it is shot. This task is usually performed by the production assistant; otherwise by the director. Logging shots achieves two things. It tells you whether you have shot everything you need to shoot and it makes finding shots that much easier when you come to edit.

This is what a typical log might look like:

WORKING TITLE :	London Tour	CLIENT: BTA		DATE: 07/10/99
PROD NO:	9903	CAM: Bob Jones SOUND: Derek Oliver		SHEET NO: 001
IN	**OUT**	**DESCRIPTION**		**COMMENT**
01.01.10	01.01.55	Shot 3 LS Pres sync intro Take 1		NG
01.02.15	01.03.02	Shot 3 LS Pres sync intro Take 2		OK USE
01.03.12	01.03.50	Shot 3 LS Pres sync intro Take 3		OK
01.04.00	01.04.30	Shot 3 CU Pres Pick-up last line Take 1		OK USE
01.04.40	01.05.05	Shot 55 MS Pres sync pay-off Take 1		OK USE

In the first column you make a note of the time code at the start of each take – the IN. The time code need only show Roll Number:Minutes:Seconds. Don't worry about frame numbers.

In the next column you note the time code at the point you cut – the OUT. If you forget to note the IN code or there isn't time to get it from the camera operator, you can always use the OUT code as a rough reference both for the end of that take and the start of the next one.

In the DESCRIPTION column you make a note of the shot size and action for the particular take, ideally with a reference to the shot number on the shooting script. You also note the take number. In the final COMMENT column you mark whether the take is OK and whether it is the one you think you will use when you edit.

In the example above you can see there are three takes of the presenter's intro shot in long shot. Take 2 was OK but you then shot a 'safety' – Take 3. You decided at the time that Take 2 was in fact better so marked that one as OK USE. You then shot a variation on Shot 3 – a close up of the Presenter delivering the last line. This is known as a **pick-up**. You are picking up on a line of the dialogue.

This is a fairly simple log. You could refine it by splitting the DESCRIPTION column into three separate columns to show shooting script number, description of the shot and the take number separately. If you then entered all the information on a computer you would be able to sort it into Shooting Script order and only show takes marked as OK USE. You would then in theory have a paper log of your finished program and a nice easy edit. But don't throw away the original log. You may still need it.

Jargon point

The tapes you shoot on are referred to as either **rushes** or **masters**. The word 'rushes' comes from the feature film world and originally meant a rush print of the previous day's shooting, processed overnight and viewed first thing in the morning to see if all the shots had worked. The word 'master' is a more accurate description but in the world of tape people also talk about an **edit master**, meaning a completed program. So to avoid confusion we shall stick to the term rushes.

Chapter 9
Shooting Rules

As we have seen earlier you will very seldom be shooting pictures in the same order as they will end up on the screen. On a single-camera shoot you will also want to create the illusion that you have a number of cameras, each shooting the same event from a number of different angles.

To do both successfully you need to understand about **eyelines** and **continuity**. The principles of both are fairly straightforward. Eyelines are about making sure that the direction in which one subject is looking and the angle and position from which they are shot match up with the way a second subject you will be cutting to is also looking and will be shot. Continuity is about making sure that a subject looks the same each time you shoot it.

Both these concepts are best explained by simple examples.

Eyelines

In this picture – a 2-shot establishing an interview – the man's eyeline is from left to right and the woman's is from right to left. In other words the man is looking right and the woman is looking left. Eyelines are always described from the camera's point of view rather than the subject's.

Profile 2-shot

You won't just be shooting the interview in this wide 2-shot. You will be shooting closer shots of both the man and the woman and perhaps other wide shots of them from different angles. There might be quite a lapse of real time between the actual shooting of each of those shots. So you need to remember that every time the camera favours the man he must be looking right and every time the camera favours the woman she must be looking left.

The reason is fairly obvious. If you get it wrong and shoot them both looking the same way, it is going to look very odd when you cut back and forth between them. They won't appear to be looking at one another. One way of avoiding this is to define what is known as **the line** – the line of action. This is an imaginary line which the camera must never cross.

The Line

In this instance the line is an imaginary line drawn between the man's eyes and the woman's eyes. The camera is south of this line and should never go anywhere north of it. If that does happen you will have 'crossed the line' and you will have shot material you cannot use. If that material happens to be all your interview questions, you may be in trouble.

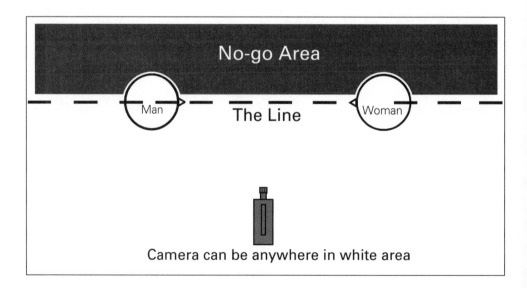

The other classic example that helps illustrate the concept of the line is a multi-camera shoot of a football match. The line in this instance is drawn from one goal mouth to the other. All your cameras must be one side only of the line; preferably the actual south side or the sun will be shining straight into your lenses.

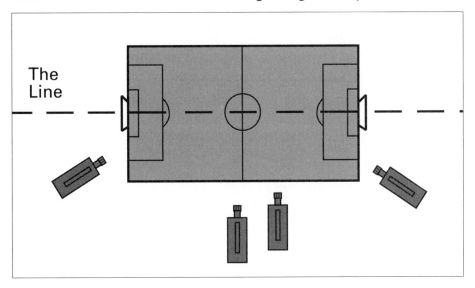

The
Line

You are going to be cutting from a wide angle shot of play to a close up of a single player with the ball. In each shot the player must be seen to be moving in the same direction. If your close-up camera was on the north side of the pitch the player with the ball would suddenly appear to have reversed direction and the viewer would be totally confused.

There are ways you can cross the line legitimately. The simplest way is via a tracking shot where the camera actually moves across the line. The viewer can see what is happening and there is nothing odd about the direction in which everyone is looking on subsequent shots. However, all subsequent shots must be shot from the new side of the line until or unless you have found a way of crossing it again.

Matching Eyelines

As well as remembering to shoot only from one side of the line, you also need to make sure that eyelines are matching. Say you are shooting two people speaking to one another and one is sitting and the other is standing. When you shoot each of their close ups the person sitting should be looking up, as if at the person standing, and the person standing should be looking down.

This may seem perfectly obvious but you may well be shooting the person who is sitting without the other subject there. You need to remember where they would have been and how that affects your subject. Unless you get it right and give each of the subjects the correct eyeline relative to the camera and to one another, either one of them could appear not to be looking directly at the other when you intercut their shots.

Exit Left, Enter Right

The principle of the line also applies where you are shooting a subject moving out of one shot and then picking them up in a subsequent shot. The rule is if they go out left, they must enter right and if they go out right, they must enter left.

A man is walking down the street towards the camera. He exits to the **right** of frame. You then want to see him going away from camera. You point the camera in the opposite direction.

He must now enter **left** of frame walking away from the camera. If he enters right of frame you have crossed the line and it will appear to the viewer that he is suddenly walking in the opposite direction.

Continuity

The continuity rule is simple to understand but not so easy to follow. It is all about watching details in a shot and making sure that when you cut, say, from a wide shot to a close up of the same scene, nothing in the picture has changed. On a multi-camera shoot where you are effectively shooting live this is seldom a problem. On a single camera shoot it often is.

Let's take a very simple example:

A

B

You want to cut from A to B

SHOOTING RULES

You have got a problem. In shot A the man has nothing in his hand. In shot B he is suddenly holding a pen.

How did this happen? You shot the single of the man at his desk (B) first as well as a whole lot more shots from that camera position. You broke for lunch. You came back, repositioned the camera looking in the opposite direction, relit the scene, stuck him back in his chair and shot your wide angle favouring the woman with the man in foreground with his back to camera (A). You forgot he was holding a pen when you shot him earlier.

The result is two shots that won't look right when cut together. So it's important to register all the details of whatever is happening in the scene you shoot first and make sure those same details are identical in all subsequent shots of the same scene. Similarly you have to watch details such as people's hair, their clothing, the position of their hands and the positioning of all props that appear in shot.

The scene you shoot first is often referred to as the **master shot**. It is the shot that governs how everything should look in all other shots of the same scene. Very often the master shot is your widest shot of a scene. It shows everything. If in all tighter shots all actions are repeated as they were performed in the master shot and all physical objects remain exactly as they were in the master, all your close ups should work. They should all cut with the master and with one another.

Very often it is worth having a Polaroid camera with you and taking a still of the master shot both at the beginning and end of the take. That way you have a ready reference to compare with when you come to shooting tighter shots from any angle. If you are really pushed you can take a look at the tape to check. But this is never a good idea. It wastes time and there is always a danger you don't spool forward again to the right point and you end up taping over something. It has happened.

Continuity nasties

☐ Person with long hair has strands sticking up on shot, smoothed down on another.

☐ Papers on desk are in one position on one shot and have moved on another.

☐ Person has their weight on one leg and head leaning one way on one shot and the other way on next shot.

☐ Man's tie is fully done up on one shot and has slipped down slightly on next.

☐ Jacket is buttoned up on one shot, unbuttoned on the next.

☐ Person's shirt or blouse changes colour from one shot to the next. Unlikely to happen but it has been known. You thought you had finished the interview but then you got them back next day because there was another vital question to ask.

☐ Cigarette is burned half-way down in first shot and a mere dog-end in the next. This is seldom a problem in a health conscious age when almost no one is ever seen smoking on television (unless you want to send a signal that this is a particularly weak and unpleasant individual).

And that's just on static shots. When there is action taking place and people are moving about in front of the camera, continuity can become even more complicated. If A and B exit shot together with A just ahead of B, they must enter the next shot in the same positions relative to one another.

Breaking the Rules

Nobody is perfect. On single camera shoots everyone has found themselves making continuity mistakes that create problems when they come to edit. On multi-camera shoots you can sometimes be forced to cross the line.

There are various ways of covering up continuity errors in editing but to do so you will need the material to do it with – something you can cut away to so that the continuity error is not noticeable. If we take the example of the man with the pen you could insert an extra shot between the two shots we saw above – a close up of him looking up. But you have still got to make sure his head is angled the same way and his expression is the same on both shots.

A solution that might just work

By the time the man is seen with the pen the audience will have forgotten that he didn't have a pen the first time they saw him. If they do notice they will think he picked it up while we were on the close up. So whatever the set up, always ensure you have shot these **cutaways** or release shots. That way you are covered.

If you are shooting dialogue between a number of people and you are worried that some of the eyelines are not going to match you can always cover yourself with a wide shot of the whole group and get everyone to repeat the dialogue. If the shot is wide enough you should be able to drop it in anywhere over the soundtrack to get yourself out of trouble.

The same principle applies on a live multi-camera shoot. If you have got your cameras into positions where you will be crossing the line if you cut from one to another the best way round it is to go via a wide shot that establishes the geography, reminds the viewer of who is talking to whom and then just do it. If possible get the wide shot camera shooting as close to the line as possible. It's not pretty but you will probably work again. If your camera is actually pointing straight down the line you can quite legitimately cross it. Say you are shooting a car race.

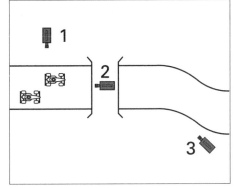

Camera 1 is on the outside of the track with the cars moving from right to left. The line is the line on which the cars are travelling. Camera 2 is on a bridge looking down on the oncoming cars. It will be on the line. Camera 3 can be on the inside of the track, the wrong side of the line.

As you cut to each camera in turn, the viewer is quite clear what is going on. But what you cannot do is cut direct from Camera 1 to Camera 3. If you do, the effect will be of two sets of cars on a collision course with one another. Fun, but not what the fans are tuning in for. Well, maybe it is but that's another story.

CHAPTER 10
SHOOTING INTERVIEWS

Interviews are a staple ingredient of most news, current affairs or documentary programs. The quality of the interviews you obtain, and the way you shoot them, can often make all the difference to the success of your production.

Interviews consist of two elements; words and pictures. First and foremost, you need to think about the words and the people who are going to say them.

Example
You are shooting a story about a little old lady who is being forced to move from her terraced house into a block of high-rise flats.

Research and Preparation

Who are You Going to Interview?

First you need to make sure that the people you are going to interview have got something worthwhile to say and that they will say it well.

Wherever possible you should meet and talk to potential interviewees before you turn up with a camera. If you can't meet them in person, talk to them on the phone. Ask yourself three things as they talk to you:

- Will this person sound OK on camera?

- Is what they are saying important?

- Is what they are saying going to add to the story?

If they are vague and rambling, or you sense they don't really know what they are talking about, thank them for talking to you but then don't waste their time or yours by shooting an interview that you are not going to use.

As a result of your research you decide you need to interview four people:

- the little old lady
- a tenant already living in a high-rise flat
- the architect who designed the flats
- the Housing Committee Chair.

What are they Going to Say?

Now you need to focus on what you want each of your interviewees to say. You will want them to speak in their own words but you also need to control the agenda. You do that through the questions. The questions are important but you should think of them as a means to an end.

The answers are what matter. Very probably you will cut the questions out of the finished piece and just cut to the interviewee for a soundbite – a short quote or statement from someone. You need to think of questions that are going to prompt the answers you want. Write them down. They'll be easier to remember and you are going to need them after you have shot the interview.

The question rule

As a general rule every question should be an 'open' question and start with one of the following words:
WHO, WHY, WHAT, WHERE, WHEN OR HOW.

Take, for example, your interview with Housing Committee Chair. This is the sort of thing that you want to happen.

> **Question:** Why are you forcing this little old lady to go and live in a high-rise flat?

Answer: We're not forcing anyone to live anywhere. The house she is living in at the moment is unsafe and requires considerable expenditure. As you know, money is tight. A number of high-rise flats are vacant, so it makes sense to rehouse people like her in them.

Question: Why are so many of the high-rise flats vacant?

Answer: People move out for all sorts of reasons. They don't always tell us why they are moving.

That wasn't bad. You've got a revealing exchange there which you could use in its entirety or as two separate soundbites. If you had used a 'closed' question and not started with the word why, this is what could happen.

Question: Are you forcing this little old lady to go and live in a high-rise flat?

Answer: No.

You can recover from that but it's not going quite how you want it to.

In the first example you achieved a number of things.

* You got a clear statement of the council's policy.

* Because you were listening to the answer, you were able to put a good follow-up question that may not have been on your list. You may not have known that a number of flats were empty. The fact that they are adds meat to your story.

* The Chair's second answer tends to suggest that the council is remote and doesn't know what is going on. Just the sort of thing you want.

* You also got self-contained soundbites that you can use on their own without the questions.

The **Who, Why, What, Where, When, How** rule isn't absolutely set in concrete and you can break it if you want to. But it's worth remembering, particularly if you are interviewing someone who either isn't that keen to be interviewed or who isn't a natural talker.

How is it Going to Look?

Interviews are not just 'talking heads'. The way you shoot them can make a significant difference to how well you are telling your story. In the preparatory stage you need to be thinking about two things; the foreground (normally the interviewee) and the background against which they will be seen.

The Background

The background for each of the interviews needs to be different. This gives your production visual variety. At the same time each of your backgrounds can make a statement that helps you tell the story.

You decide to shoot the interview with the tenant in their flat looking out over the rest of the city.

As she is describing what life is like high on the 17th floor your audience has an additional visual sense of that by sharing the tenant's daily view.

The little old lady is going to be pictured in her living room.

Quite apart from what the little old lady says in words, what the audience is seeing is her home which she obviously cares for.

The architect will be seen with a high-rise towering up behind him. Your interview with the architect will be saying, visually, 'this is how he saw it on paper as he drew the building from the ground up'. You might also want to shoot him inside one of the flats and ask him whether he would like to live in one of these places.

Your interview with the Housing Committee Chair will be shot in the council chamber.

Visually, the background is saying to your audience 'this is where the decision was taken to build these flats'.

Each of the backgrounds is saying something visually to your audience. Choosing the right background can be as important as choosing the right person to interview.

Background Recces

Always try and recce interview locations in advance of shooting. Check that the background you want is going to be available when you want it. Don't just turn up at the local council offices and expect to be able to shoot in the council chamber without having asked someone first.

If you are shooting exteriors, make sure the sun will be shining in the right direction at the time of day you will be shooting. Think about any potential sound problems. Unless you are making a video about aircraft noise, avoid shooting interviews under the flight path of an international airport.

Backgrounds Checklist

☐ Are the backgrounds different enough from one another?

☐ Is each of the backgrounds adding visually to the story?

☐ Will the backgrounds be available when you want them?

☐ Do any of the locations present sound or lighting problems?

Creating the Background You Want

You may well find that the background you want either doesn't exist or what is available isn't going to look that good on camera. There are two ways round this:

Chromakey

Shoot the interview against a plain coloured screen and key in your own background using Chromakey. We touched on this technique in Chapter 8. It can be very effective.

BUT

- You have to bring your own coloured screen with you, though there are collapsible ones.

- Both screen and interviewee have to be evenly and carefully lit.

- Even if the lighting is perfect, there is always a risk of giving your interviewee's hair a blue rinse effect.

- You won't know whether it is going to work until your final online edit.

- Your interviewee must not wear anything the same colour as your screen.

Dressing the Set

Rearrange a room and its furnishings to get the effect you are after. In drama productions this is known as 'dressing the set' and the term is used on all types of shoots. Normally you would use items already there but you might want to import 'props' like a vase of flowers. For example, the little old lady interview:

This is what the room looks like normally.

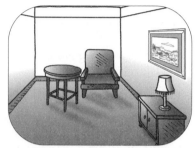

This is what the shot would look like if you do nothing. All you can see is the back of the armchair and a blank wall. It could be anywhere and it says nothing visually. There is no depth to the picture. Because the chair is still slap up against the wall you won't have been able to put in a backlight.

This is the shot you want. Your background reflects a scene of comfortable domesticity. You have had to create it by grouping and arranging objects so that they compose an image that the camera – and your audience – can take it in at once.

To achieve that, you've had to move things about. The armchair has been moved away from the wall, the occasional table has been moved closer to the armchair. You've placed a family photograph on the table. You've moved the picture on the wall and lowered it and you've placed a table lamp in the background; it's actually standing on a pile of telephone directories.

Set Dressing Checklist

☐ Don't shoot interviewees up against walls.

☐ Create some depth in the shot.

☐ Make sure you don't have things growing out of people's heads. The video picture doesn't have a third dimension so if there is a potted palm directly behind the subject it could look odd.

☐ Try and add colour, particularly in offices, e.g. put coloured ring binders on a shelf in the background.

☐ Allow time for dressing the set.

The Foreground

Normally your interviewee will be in the foreground of your shot. There are three decisions you need to take about how you shoot the foreground. You must decide on:

- The angle
- The eyeline
- The shot size(s).

None of these is difficult as long as you follow a few simple rules.

The Angle

In this case we are not talking about the lens angle – wide or tight. We are talking about the angle of the camera relative to the subject you are shooting. In general on interviews the angle should be as tight as possible. Your interviewee should be looking just off camera so that the audience can see as much of the interviewee's face as possible. People 'talk' with their eyes. So show both eyes. The simplest way to ensure this is to place the person asking the questions as close to the camera as possible.

Person asking questions is close to camera

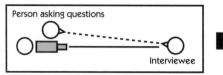

The result is a tight angle showing as much as possible of the interviewee's face

Person asking questions is too far away from camera

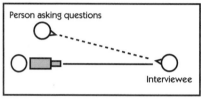

The result is a three-quarter profile which doesn't communicate so well with the audience

Alternatively, you might choose to shoot the interviewee in full profile. This can be very effective for certain people and certain situations, particularly if you have the luxury of shooting with two cameras and you are shooting a program that consists of one long interview. However, it is not advised for short videos such as

Full profile

news and current affairs reports or corporate videos. Most company chairmen have fairly unflattering profiles. They'll blame you, not their mothers, for the way they look. You might win an award but you've also lost a client.

The Eyeline

The choice is simple. Are you going to shoot the interviewee looking camera left or looking camera right?

If the production includes more than one interview, you may want to cut between them. If they are all looking the same way, they won't cut as well as if they are looking in contrasting directions. If you have got two people with opposing views on a subject, you are making the point visually by shooting them with opposing eyelines. Bear in mind, too, that a particular background may affect the direction in which an interviewee is facing.

So before you decide on the eyeline, you need to answer three questions:

- In what **order** will people first be appearing in the finished production? (This will not necessarily be the order in which you actually shoot their interviews.)

- Which interviews are you likely to want to **intercut**?

- Will any **backgrounds** determine the eyeline?

For the high-rise flats story, the answers are as follows:

The Order

You are already fairly certain that the interviewees will be seen first in the following order:

1   The little old lady

2   The high-rise tenant

3   The architect

4   The Chair.

Intercutting

You are also fairly certain that you will want to intercut the little old lady and the Chair. So these two each need to have opposing eyelines.

Effect of Backgrounds

You have recced all the locations and you know that the background for the architect will work best if he is looking left with the flats rising up on the left of shot. The other three backgrounds will work equally well whatever the eyeline. So put camera left beside the architect:

1   The little old lady
2   The high-rise tenant
3   The architect   Camera left
4   The Chair

Now you can fill in the other three, alternating each one:

1   The little old lady   Camera left
2   The high-rise tenant   Camera right
3   The architect   Camera left
4   The Chair   Camera right

You can check it is going to work with a simple storyboard:

1 Little old lady looking left   *2 High-rise tenant looking right*   *3 The Architect looking left*   *4 The Chair looking right*

Shooting them like this also means that intercutting the little old lady and the Chair is going to work successfully. There is a degree of luck involved as you never quite know how you are going to intercut interviews. But if you have shot half your interviews with one eyeline and the other half with the opposing eyeline, you will always have a greater number of options.

 TIP

Before you start shooting each interview make a note of the eyeline. Is the subject looking camera right or camera left?

The Shot Size(s)

If you know exactly how you are going to use an interview you might choose to hold one shot size throughout to match other interviews. If you are not quite sure what you are going to use, and want to keep your editing options open, it is often a good idea to vary the sizes for each answer. As a general rule it is best to zoom in or out while a question is being asked. If you know there is going to be one particular crunch answer, you might want to go into a close-up or big close-up.

Try and decide beforehand what the pattern is likely to be. It should be discussed and agreed between camera and director. There's a full description of shot sizes and what they are called in Chapter 8. If you think you might want a close-up at a particular moment that hasn't been prearranged, arrange a discreet signalling system with the camera operator; one that isn't going to distract the interviewee or result in jogging the camera operator's arm.

Checks and Chairs

Three final points to watch for:

- Make sure interviewees are not wearing jackets with stripey checks. What's known as a Prince of Wales check is the worst. It's made up of lots of lines which the camera can't handle. On your picture the lines will dance up and down or 'strobe'.

- The collars of men's jackets tend to ride up when they are seated. Get them to pull the back of their jackets well down before they start.

- Try and avoid having an interviewee sit in a swivel chair. Under the strain they will tend to waggle about. This is irritating and distracting. If you are forced to use a swivel chair, warn the person not to move about.

The Shoot

Setting Up

Allow plenty of time for setting up your equipment, for lighting and dressing the set. You are likely to need anything between 30 minutes and an hour at the location before you are ready to shoot, particularly if you have to park, unload equipment, get past the receptionist and take the lift to the fifth floor.

Try and arrange for the interviewee to join you once you expect to be ready. This isn't just a matter of courtesy. If the interviewee is hanging around waiting for you to get ready, he or she is likely to get nervous, irritated or bored and you may not get the best interview out of them.

Just before you start shooting, disconnect or redirect the telephone and make sure people in any nearby rooms know you are shooting. Ask them to be quiet.

Shooting the Interview

So, the camera is all set up, you're happy with the background and the eyeline, you've made a note of the eyeline and you've worked out your questions. You're ready to go. Or you think you are.

But there's a problem ...

Councillor Bloggs, the Housing Committee Chair, has just arrived. He is shorter than you thought he would be. The shot doesn't quite work any more and you need to adjust the tripod. He's nervous. And bald. His brow is perspiring and the top of his head is shining under your lights. He also wants to know what you are going to ask him.

Remember those interpersonal skills? You are going to need them. You are also going to need a powder puff. It's going to take about another five minutes to sort out all these little problems.

Run through the questions by all means but don't let Councillor Bloggs rehearse his answers if you can help it. It's actually in his own interest that he doesn't. If he is any kind of politician at all he will already have thought about what he is going to say. You want his answers to be as natural and spontaneous as possible. His performance will be far better if you haven't both rehearsed the interview beforehand.

Once you've gone through the questions, get him talking about something else. Ask him about his used car dealership, his holidays, his family. Chat away about yourself. Tell him about some of the celebs you've worked with. He'll love it. Put him at ease and get his mind off the interview. He'll snap back into gear when you want him to. This isn't just because he is a politician. Everyone who is worth interviewing has what you want to hear somewhere in their heads. Your skill lies in getting it out of them.

At this stage you may be wondering – why are you telling me all this? I'm the director and all this stuff is for reporters. Two reasons: you may well be doing all this yourself because you don't have a reporter and if you do have one you need to make sure this is how they handle the situation. Everyone on the team has a part to play in sorting out any problems as quickly as possible and doing what they can to make the interviewee feel comfortable.

Why has the same electrician lit the Queen's Christmas broadcast for the past twenty years? Not just because he's good at lighting. It's because he makes her laugh.

So now you really are ready to go. The golden rule is silence – from everyone except the interviewer and interviewee. Everyone except the interviewer should keep out of the interviewee's eyeline.

Everyone on the production team should be listening carefully to what the interviewee is saying, particularly the director. Are you getting what you want? Is it clear? Is it concise? If it isn't concise, are there nuggets there you can use? If there are, will they cut? If need be, make discreet notes. They'll help you decide which questions and answers you want to re-shoot. Make a note too of the questions as they are asked.

If you're not happy with the way an interview is going, do you stop shooting or do you let it run its course and then have another go? There's no hard and fast rule. A lot will depend on how you think the interviewee will react. If you stop the interview, will they be demoralised or will they be relieved and grateful? You will need to take a view on what kind of person you are dealing with. If you are directing and working with an experienced reporter, the interview will have to be going very badly indeed before you step in and halt the proceedings. Even then your reporter is unlikely to buy you a drink that evening. Assuming the shoot has gone as planned and the interview is over, make a note of the time code in the OUT column of your log.

Cutaways

If you are working with a reporter, you may now want to shoot some cutaways. A cutaway is any shot that you cut away to from the master shot of the interviewee speaking. Cutaway shots of the reporter allow you to edit the interview to look like a conversation between two people. They also provide you with escape shots so that you can edit the sound without the picture jumping.

There are four basic reporter cutaways:

- 2-shot favouring the interviewee (usually mute).

- Single sync shot of the reporter asking the questions.

- Single mute shot of the reporter appearing to listen – 'noddies'.

- 2-shot favouring the reporter (shot either sync with the reporter asking the questions or mute with the reporter appearing to listen).

2-shot favouring the interviewee

Set up this 2-shot while the camera is still favouring the interviewee. Position

2-shot favouring the interviewee (usually mute)

the camera so that it only sees the reporter's jaw movement, not lip movement. The reporter should be talking as if asking questions. The interviewee should only listen and not respond. The interviewee's facial expression should be as it was when being actually interviewed.

When you edit, you can use this shot with the soundtrack of a question being asked from the original interview. The sound will be wild. As long as the camera cannot see the reporter's lips, it will look as if sound and picture are in sync. You can use this shot if you want to cut an answer and go to a question. You can also use it to introduce the interviewee.

If you have to move the camera to get this wider shot, make sure you don't cross the line.

Single sync shot of the reporter asking the questions

This shot (and the final two shots) are also known as **reverse angles** or **reverses**. This means they are shot from the reverse or opposite camera angle of the interview master shot – as if you had a second camera.

There is a **golden rule** for reverse angle cutaways of the reporter. The reporter *must* be looking in the opposite direction from the way the interviewee was facing. This sounds fairly obvious but shooting reverse angle cutaways is going to involve a new camera set-up. Nine times out of ten you don't leave the reporter sitting where they were for the interview and simply move the camera round to face them. You may want to move the reporter into a position with a better background. It's even possible that you are shooting the interview on one day and the cutaways on another.

Reverse angle

In the new set-up which way should the reporter be looking?

You shot Councillor Bloggs looking camera right. You *must* shoot the reporter looking camera left.

You'll always get it right so long as you've made a note of the original interview eyeline and you shoot the reporter looking in the opposite direction.

If you are shooting sync sound of the questions being asked, the phrasing of the question should be the same as in the original interview. This is why it is important to note down questions as they are asked during the interview shoot.

If you varied the size of shot on the interviewee, shoot the reverse angle cutaways in a variety of sizes so that they will match.

Single mute shot of the reporter appearing to listen – 'noddies'

The set-up, eyeline and shot sizes for the noddies will be exactly the same as for the previous shot.

You can use the noddies to cut from one part of an answer to another part of an answer.

It's a good idea to get the reporter to give you various different expressions on the noddies but don't overdo it. If the interview was a load of fun then the reporter ought to be smiling on some of the noddies.

2-shot favouring the reporter

You will only be able to shoot this if the interviewee is co-operative and can spare the time. Again it is a reverse angle shot so the reporter must be shot looking in the opposite direction from the interviewee.

2-shot favouring the reporter

If you simply shoot it mute for use as a noddy, get the interviewee to talk to the reporter but make sure the camera can only see jaw movement, not lip movement. The reporter should just be listening or reacting. You can of course also shoot it sync with the questions being asked.

And Finally . . .

Shoot a buzz track – around a minute of the ambient sound in the location. You'll find this comes in very useful to smooth over the sound on any edits.

That's the interview shoot completed but you're not quite done yet. If you are shooting in someone's home or office and you've rearranged all the furniture, put it back where it was. It makes life a lot easier for the next crew that wants to come and shoot there. Tell anyone who has been quiet next door that they can now talk normally.

Thank the interviewee and anyone else who has helped you.

Interview Flowchart

| Select interviewees |
| Prepare questions |
| Select backgrounds |
| Decide eyelines |
| Dress set |
| Decide shot sizes |

PREPARATION

| Silence |
| Listen |
| Notes |
| Log |
| Cutaways |
| Clear up – Thank you |

SHOOT

Chapter 11
Shooting Action

There are two types of action sequence you are likely to want to shoot. In the one you are able to direct what is happening so that it works for the camera. In the other you have no control over the event and have to go with what is happening. In this chapter we will look at each separately and then move on to a few tricks and treats.

Directed Action

Planning Checklist

Before you shoot a sequence of directed action you must plan ahead:

☐ decide what you want to see happening

☐ work out how you will shoot it

☐ decide how the shots involved will cut together

☐ decide the order in which you will shoot them

☐ communicate what you want to see happening and how you want it covered

What do You Want to see Happening?

We'll go back to a simple example we have already touched on. You want to see a woman walking past a For Sale sign and walking up to the front door of the house. She rings the doorbell, the owner comes to the door. They chat on the doorstep.

How Will You Shoot It?

The simplest way of shooting this is by starting on the For Sale sign, zooming out gently as the woman walks past it, panning with her as she walks up the garden path and letting the rest of the action take place on a wide shot of the path and house.

It is also the most boring way of doing it. Apart from the brief moment we see the woman in profile walking past the sign, for most of the shot all we see of her is her uninteresting back view. Added to which the action takes too long to happen and on the wide shot the audience won't see much of what is happening at the front door. So should you zoom in with the woman as she walks up towards it? Ugly. Too much camera movement. Zoom out, pan, zoom in. Classic home movie-style overuse of the zoom.

The answer is to break the action down and then decide how each element is to be shot in such a way that the separate shots will all cut together. Make a list either on paper or in your head.

Breakdown of the action

1   The whole scene.

2   Woman walks past For Sale sign.

3   Woman walks up to front door.

4   Woman rings doorbell.

5   Owner comes to the door.

6   Woman and owner chat on the doorstep.

Now you can decide on how each of those elements is going to be shot:

1	Whole scene	Master shot – wide shot of walk
2	Woman walks past For Sale sign	Static mid shot from same position as master shot
3	Woman walks up to front door	Reverse angle LS woman walking up path
4	Woman goes to ring doorbell	Mid shot woman going to ring doorbell – shot from path facing house
5	Woman rings doorbell	Close up finger on doorbell – shot from path
6	Woman waits at door	Cutaway woman waiting at door
7	Owner comes to the door	Mid shot of door opening – shot from path. Man and woman chat, camera favouring man
8	They chat on the doorstep	Man and woman chat, camera favouring woman

This is what you want your sequence to look like when you cut it together:

Will it Cut Together?

In theory it will. Your storyboard proves that it is going to work. The only way it is likely to go wrong is if you make a mistake in the way you actually shoot it.

Deciding the shooting order

In this case the order in which you shoot each shot is fairly straight-forward. It is the same as the order in which you will actually cut the shots together – but with three exceptions, Shots 5, 6 and 7.

Shot 7 is in fact a continuation of Shot 4 so it makes sense to shoot them both at the same time and leave Shot 5, the close up of the doorbell being rung, as the last shot you do from outside the house. That still leaves Shot 6, the cutaway of the woman waiting on the doorstep which it will be best to do after you have set up inside the house for Shot 8.

If you were actually doing this on paper rather than in your head, you could put an alphabetic reference beside each shot or camera set-up to show the order in which each will be shot:

1	Whole scene	A	Master shot – wide shot of walk
2	Woman walks past For Sale sign	B	Static mid shot from same position as master shot
3	Woman walks up to front door	C	Reverse angle LS woman walking up path
4	Woman goes to rings doorbell	D	Mid shot woman going to ring doorbell – shot from path facing house
5	Woman rings doorbell	F	Close up finger on doorbell – shot from path

6	Woman waits at door	H	Cutaway woman waiting at door
7	Owner comes to the door	E	Mid shot of door opening – shot from path. Man and woman chat, camera favouring man
8	They chat on the doorstep	G	Man and woman chat, camera favouring woman

If this seems complicated, don't worry. It is a lot harder to work out or to follow on paper than to do in practice. The guiding principle it that you should always complete all the shots you need from one camera set-up before you move on to the next. This isn't just because everybody gets fed up with having to move kit unnecessarily back to a previous set-up. It is also a question of continuity. You are very unlikely to be able to recreate the exact look you had before, particularly if lighting is involved.

Communication

Now you have worked out what you are going to do it is vital that everyone involved knows what has been going on in your head all this time and what you expect them to do to make it happen successfully.

If you are directing the sequence, talk it all through with your camera operator and sound recordist, explain how you think it is going to work and ask them if they foresee any problems. If you have been behaving reasonably towards them so far they will point out anything you may have overlooked and may suggest ways of doing one or more shots in an even more imaginative way than you have thought of. Part of a director's skill is in getting everyone on the team to contribute positively. If you have failed to strike up a good relationship, people will just do as you tell them. If that means you are making elementary errors then that is your problem. But let's not dwell on that. This is a happy shoot. You have been buying your share of the drinks and your idea of meal breaks involves more than chewing on sandwiches as you race down the motorway to complete an unrealistic schedule.

Communication doesn't just mean the director talking. It also involves listening. The camera operator and the sound recordist will have questions. The recordist may want to know if you need to hear the dialogue on the doorstep when you are on the long shot. If so, it may be necessary to rig up radio mikes. The camera operator may want to know whether you want to see into the house when the door is open. If you do, it may be necessary to light the interior. Try and sort all these issues out before you start shooting.

You also need to brief the woman who is going to be walking up the path and the homeowner. Explain what you want them to do and how you want them to do it. Do you want the woman to be walking briskly or casually? Should the homeowner be glad to see her, is he expecting her, does he know her or is he wary of her? Make it clear to both of them that you will be getting them to do everything a number of times – because you will be shooting the action from a variety of angles. Impress upon them that each time they perform a bit of the action they should do it the same way as they did it the first time, i.e. on the master shot. These points apply whether you are working with professional actors or members of the public.

Shooting

Now you are ready to shoot A, the master shot. You will be on a wide angle. The woman will walk into shot past the For Sale sign. The camera will pan with her as she walks up the path and rings the bell. The door will open, the householder will appear and you will see them chatting in long shot. The woman will be carrying a clipboard. She will be travelling from left to right.

The Line

The line you establish on the master shot is a curving line from the woman to the front door. The camera is to the right of the line. On all subsequent shots it must stay to the right of the line.

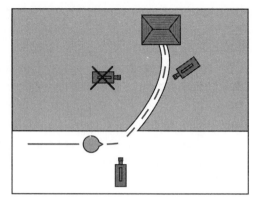

Cueing

You are going to need to co-ordinate the action and the camera movement. At the start of the master shot the woman needs to walk into shot. She needs to be moving at a regular pace rather than looking as if she has just set off from a standing start. So start her off a few paces to the left of the edge of frame and rehearse the shot. If it looks right give the woman a '**mark**' – a piece of tape stuck to the pavement where you want her to start from. If it doesn't quite work shift the start position and the mark as required.

Ideally everything should happen from the one cue – the director calling 'Action'. But in this case you want a two-second pause between the doorbell ringing and door opening. Brief the homeowner to stand immediately behind the closed front door and to open it on a count of two after he has heard the doorbell. 'That's all very well,' he says 'but I'm afraid the bell's not working'. Get him to stand in his front room just back from the window so he can see the woman approaching the front door. The room isn't lit so the camera won't see him. Time how long it takes him to get to the front door and work out at what point in the woman's walk you will need to give him a signal to move to the front door. Agree what the signal is going to be. Make a note that you will need a sound effect of door bell to dub in later. (Better still, record one in the course of this shoot. It saves a lot of hunting around for effects disks.)

Now rehearse the full shot so that the woman gets her walk right, the camera operator is able to see if the pan works satisfactorily and the door opens on cue. It all works. Pity you didn't say

'Rehearse-record' and shoot the rehearsal.

Never mind. You are now ready to shoot. You're in luck. It works. First time. Fantastic.

In the same set-up you shoot B – the closer shot of the woman walking past the sign. You may want to use this to open the cut sequence.

On to the next set up C – the reverse angle long shot of the woman walking up the path.

What do you need to check?

☐ Have you crossed the line?

☐ Is the continuity all right?

The Line: If the camera is still to the right of the line you are all right. On the master shot the woman started off travelling from left to right. On this shot she will still be travelling from left to right. You have not crossed the line. This is going to cut.

Continuity: Was the woman carrying anything on the master shot. Yes. She had a clipboard. Which hand was it in? How was she holding it? Were any papers sticking out of it?

Shooting Action

Once the camera is set up and you have decided on the shot give the woman a new start mark a few paces back from the point at which you think you will be cutting into the shot. This both ensures she is up to speed and gives you more choice when you edit. Make sure she walks past the camera and does not look at it.

That works OK. This is going great. While we're in this set-up let's pop in an extra shot we didn't talk about earlier – a close up of the woman walking towards camera. Your camera operator doesn't look all that excited. What you are after is a travelling close up of the woman walking up the path. You want the shot size to remain constant throughout so the camera is going to have to be gently zooming back with her. The camera also needs to be steadily tilting up and panning slightly to keep her in the frame. But what really makes this shot tricky is the fact that the woman is getting ever closer to the camera while you are on a relatively narrow lens. It is going to be difficult to keep her in sharp focus all the time. This is the moment you wish you had a camera assistant to pull focus or had invested in a dolly and track to do the shot. Still, this isn't a shot you desperately need. The sequence works without it. So you give it a whirl and decide there might be a couple of seconds of it that you can use.

Alternative scenario: you spend (waste) half an hour getting it nearly right and then give up. It is now half past one. No one has eaten since breakfast and the sound recordist is complaining that tummy rumbles are being picked up on the soundtrack. You have got the rest of this sequence to shoot and you have to be at a location 20 miles away by three o'clock. You are learning the hard way that program making isn't just about being creative. It's also about managing time and people. But we digress . . .

Now you're going to turn the camera round to face the door and shoot the woman walking towards it, ringing the bell, waiting a moment. We'll then see the door being opened by the homeowner and record their dialogue – the shots you marked as D and E.

For D you start the woman off out of shot a few paces behind the camera so that you see her entering the shot. Again you will need to arrange some method of cueing the homeowner to open the door.

That works fine. So does E, the 2-shot from the same direction of the two of them chatting. The clipboard is still in the same hand as we have seen it on the previous shots, or is it?

Now you can shoot F, the close up of the woman's finger pressing the doorbell. Well, yes, except that she's had the clipboard in her right hand and that's the side the doorbell is on. You realised that would be a problem when you shot the mid shot of her approaching

the door and you got her to transfer the clipboard to her left hand just as she approached the door. You also remembered to keep it in her left hand when you were on the shot of her chatting with the homeowner. And you are going to remember that it will have to be in her left hand when you shoot looking out from the house. So not a problem.

Whenever you are shooting a close up of a hand or finger doing something, it is always best to start with the hand right out of shot. You then want it to move smoothly into the shot, do its stuff and then move smartly out of shot. Again this makes editing a lot easier.

SHOOTING ACTION

If the hand is already partly in shot or comes in hesitantly you won't get a clean movement and the edit will look messy. Check for grubby fingernails. They look very nasty on a big close up.

So now you're done outside. This is a good moment to break for lunch. The homeowner is happy for you to stow your gear in his hall while you are gone. That's where you are going to be working next.

Back from lunch you set up to shoot from the hall. It's a bit of a squeeze in there with at least three of you, the camera and the homeowner. It's an hour since you were last shooting – from the other direction. Your mind has been wandering over lunch. You've had a couple of drinks. This is the moment you are in greatest danger of crossing the line. Because of the cramped conditions the easiest way to get a 2-shot is to have the camera looking over the homeowner's right shoulder. Where is the line? Which way is the woman looking if you do this? She will be looking right. Which way was the homeowner looking on the reverse? He was looking right. Shoot it this way and you will be in trouble. And remember which hand the woman's clipboard should now be in.

You shift the camera so that you are looking over the homeowner's left shoulder. Shot G now works.

You shoot it and then with the camera in the same position but with the door wide open and the homeowner out of the way you shoot H, the closer shot of the woman standing at the door waiting for it to open.

Sequence shot and completed. But while you are here you realise there is another shot you could do which will cut nicely into the sequence. You could get the woman to walk straight up the path towards the camera, switch the clipboard from her right to left hand, ring the bell and stand and wait. Because the camera will be straight on to her, warn her not to look at camera. If she is a real person, as opposed to an actor, her eyes may well flick towards the camera at some point. Check carefully as you shoot that this doesn't happen.

So now you have shot a complete action sequence. It might have taken you around an hour to shoot. It will probably end up as around 20 seconds on the screen.

Checklist for shooting action under your control

☐ Take control of the situation

☐ Plan the sequence in your head or on paper before you shoot

☐ Communicate fully and clearly

☐ Check the line on every set-up

☐ Check continuity on every set-up

☐ Remember that separate set-ups all take time

Action As It Is Happening

Very often you won't be able to take control of an event and direct the action as you want it to happen for the camera. You will have to go with the action as it is happening. News cameras have to do this all the time, though what you see on the news is not always as spontaneous as it seems. If you ever see soldiers in a war zone advancing towards the camera it is a sure bet this is either a staged shot or the camera operator is a suicidal maniac.

Whatever the situation, you need to remember two things when you shoot action as it is happening:

- it must be clear to the viewer what is going on – the pictures must tell a story and not just be irrelevant 'wallpaper' to cover commentary

- try and shoot from a variety of angles and with a variety of shot sizes so as to increase your editing options.

If possible try and find out what is likely to happen before you start shooting. With a production process in a factory this is easy. Take a look at it, decide what you want to shoot and how it might cut together. Then do it. With a bit of luck it will all be happening exactly the same when you come to shoot it. Because the action is endlessly repeating itself your continuity problems are automatically solved. Unless of course you haven't checked and you find you get half your shots done and the operator then tells you that's all the widgets made for today. He's got to set the machine up for something else now.

Once you have established he is going to be turning out widgets for the next half hour or so, you need to do a bit of quick planning:

- what shots are going to tell the story?

- what shots are going to look best?

- what order are you going to shoot them in?

- how will they cut together?

In other words there is a planning process – just as there was for a sequence under your control.

To let the viewer know what is going on it is always best to shoot a wide shot of the scene – **an establisher**. If possible try and make this a high angle shot. High angle shots both have a dramatic quality and allow you to see more of what is going on.

Shooting from a variety of different angles and in a variety of different sizes achieves two things:

• it makes the sequence visually interesting

• it increases the chances that it will all cut together.

To make absolutely sure that it will all cut together always give yourself some **escape shots**. In this example the most obvious escape shot is a cutaway close up of the machine operator. It may be a good shot in its own right – showing concentration, dedication to the job or utter boredom with it. But from an editing point of view it is also a shot you can insert between two other shots which otherwise might not cut together smoothly.

For example, if you have got two wide shots shot from a similar angle but with slightly different action going on in each of them, you won't be able to cut from one directly to the other. But if you have got an escape shot or cutaway to put between them no one will notice the difference.

 TIP

Shoot plenty of cutaway escape shots.

The Line and Continuity

You won't have a lot of control over the line and continuity when you are shooting action as it is happening but you still need to be thinking about them. Try and cover yourself with escape shots that will get you out of any trouble later. You might be covering a St Patrick's Day parade through New York. You'll be running ahead of the parade to get different shots and you might find you are forced to shoot from different sides of the street. If you haven't shot cutaways of the crowd watching or a few landmark buildings you could end up making the parade appear to march back on itself. If this is going out on British television you won't be making a very positive contribution to Anglo-Irish relations.

Use Both Eyes

If you are shooting an event outside your control the camera operator needs to use both eyes – one on what is happening in the viewfinder, the other on what is happening elsewhere that might be offering the next or an even better shot. If a camera operator and director are working together the director needs to be doing the same – keeping one eye on what material is being acquired and what else is offering itself.

But both need to be careful. When you are shooting the St Patrick's Day parade the director is unlikely to have a monitor and will have to make an estimate of what is being shot. It can be very irritating for camera operators to have a director constantly whispering in their ear as they shoot (quite apart from any less than fresh breath issues). It can also be counter-productive. Many is the time a director has said 'Quick, pan left to the drummer' just as the camera operator has focused on a pleasing shot of the majorettes. He pans, loses the majorettes and can't find the drummer.

The director should try and sort out what type of shots are wanted before shooting and leave the camera operator to get on with it.

Sound

The parade provides a classic example of a sound problem that occurs when you are covering this type of event. If you are constantly cutting and restarting recording you will end up with a disjointed soundtrack. Given the content of the sound is music being played by the band you will end up with a bit of mess when you editing. If you are going to be putting voice over the music it may not matter that the audience cannot actually hear a continuous tune or melody.

There are several ways round this:

1   Keep the camera running throughout the time you are shooting so you record a continuous soundtrack to which you edit pictures later. But this won't work if you are moving around to get good camera positions. The sound recordist will not be able to cope.

2   Record a whole musical number wild either before or after you shoot for pictures and then cut everything to it.

3   Record continuous sound separately on a second recorder.

4   Dub in a music track from disk later but then you won't hear any of the other actuality sound – people laughing, cheering, etc.

Option 3 is the best method but it has cost implications. Option 2 is what happens in most cases. On a single camera shoot this is probably what the sound recordist will want to do and will suggest.

Shooting Ratio

Whenever possible you should try and keep your shooting ratio within reasonable bounds. Shooting ratio is a measurement of the amount of tape you shoot against the amount that actually ends up on the screen. If you shoot sixty minutes of tape (two 30 minute rolls) for a 10 minute program your ratio will be 6:1. Shooting ratios are less critical on tape than they are on film. The cost of stock is lower per minute and there are no processing costs. On film anything more than a 10:1 ratio is starting to put a strain on your budget.

Because tape is relatively inexpensive many people shooting on tape tend not to worry too much about shooting ratios. But money isn't the only consideration. If you shoot too much material you will have to spend many frustrating hours in the edit, even with a good log, hunting through it to find what you want. And if you have to put your program together quickly you may not have the time to do that.

There are camera operators and directors who use the camera like a spray gun and who proudly boast that they just squirt off shots and hope that they will end up with something they can use. There are also camera operators who always keep running between takes. There is also one who thinks you need to run the camera for ten minutes to line up a simple static shot that is only going to last three seconds on the screen. Incredibly, some of these people enjoy life-long careers in the industry. With a bit of luck one day they'll get found out.

Tricks and Treats

There are all kinds of ways that you can create exciting and expensive visual effects when you edit. There are also ways you can trick the eye to achieve visual treats when you shoot – with a little care and at no extra expense.

Builds

Let's say you want a series of objects to build up in shot. You would shoot the build in reverse. In other words you start with all the items in place, lock off the camera, start to record, keep the camera running and then carefully remove each item in the reverse order that they will appear. You then cut all the shots together in the opposite order to the order in which they were shot.

Why do it this way? Why not just put each item in place in order? The answer is that by shooting the end frame first you know everything is in exactly the position you want it. It is also physically easier to remove an object without disturbing any of the other objects than it is to place them in. If any one of the objects does get disturbed the build is not going to work and you will have to start again from the beginning.

When you are doing this it is vital that the camera remains rock steady. Any floor tremors will affect the picture so make sure people aren't walking about close by. Whoever is removing the objects will throw shadows so make sure they step well back from the shot each time.

Time Lapse

You can also build activity in one apparently continuous shot. For example, you might want to show waiters preparing tables in a restaurant, see the restaurant filling up with people, see them enjoying their meals, the restaurant then emptying of people and the waiters clearing up at the end of the day. The actual process might take about three hours. You are going to condense it into about ten seconds by setting up a wide, locked-off shot of the whole scene and then running the camera continuously for a minute or so to capture each of the segments of the action. When you edit you put together about a second or two from each segment in sequence dissolving between each shot.

Appear–Disappear

You can also use the time lapse technique to make people appear or disappear from a shot. The only problem is that the people who stay in the shot must freeze their positions as the person appearing or disappearing moves in or out and takes up position. They must then unfreeze themselves on cue. It has been known to work.

Mirrors

Think about starting a shot where the image is in fact reflected in a mirror, in water or any other reflective surface and then revealing this to the audience. There's no real reason for doing this except that it often looks good. Which is a very good reason for doing anything. But don't get carried away with it. You can have too much a good thing. Lighting mirror shots can be tricky and you must check and double-check you are not seeing anything you shouldn't – lighting stands, flight cases, etc.

Slow Motion and Fast Motion

In the days when everything was shot on film this was known as shooting **overcranked** or **undercranked**. If you wanted a slow motion shot you ran the camera at a speed faster (overcranked) than normal. When you ran the film on an editing machine or projector at normal speed the action all appeared to slow down. An undercranked shot resulted in fast motion.

With today's technology you achieve the same effect in the online edit. However, in the edit all you are actually doing is slowing down or speeding up the rate at which your play-in tape is running. The quality is never quite as good as if you had in fact shot it on film and altered the camera speed. So if your production demands a lot of slow motion you can make a strong case for shooting on film. You may never want to go back to tape.

CHAPTER 12
MULTI-CAMERA SHOOTS

There are two types of multi-camera shoot: a program shot in the studio and an outside broadcast (OB). The roles people perform and the techniques involved are very similar for both. But there are two important differences between any multi-camera shoot and a single-camera location shoot.

The first major difference between a multi-camera shoot and a single-camera location shoot is the number of people involved. In theory a single camera unit can consist of just one person fulfilling the roles of director, camera operator, sound recordist and reporter. On a multi-camera shoot the team consists of camera operators, sound crew, lighting crew, the vision mixer, vision control, engineers, tape operators, the designer, set builders, costume, make up, the floor manager and assistants, the production team and the on-air talent – the presenters.

On a single-camera shoot you can risk just turning up and hoping it will happen – or making it happen. A multi-camera shoot always requires a high degree of planning, co-ordination, teamwork and communication.

The other major difference is that multi-camera shoots are shot either live or 'as live'. In other words you record the whole program or segments of it as it will be shown, cutting between shots and mixing sound as you go. Multi-camera shooting calls for instant decision-making and fast reflexes.

The Set-Up

Before we look at the process, we'll run through the set up and see who and what you will be working with.

The most basic television studio consists of two separate areas – the studio floor itself and a suite of control rooms, more commonly referred to as the **gallery**. Production, lighting and sound may occupy separate galleries. You might also have separate areas close by for make-up, dressing rooms and the **green room** where you stick guests until they are needed.

Studio

The studio will normally have a permanent lighting rig in the ceiling. To allow maximum lighting flexibility the studio ceiling needs to be anywhere between 15 and 50 feet high. Two or three of the walls will consist of a continuous curved **cyc** or clyclorama made of either fabric or plaster. Ideally the cyc curves both at the corners and where it meets the floor. The floor needs to be an absolutely smooth, painted surface. It will usually need to be repainted before every production. The whole studio floor area must be fully soundproofed.

On the studio floor equipment is likely to consist of the cameras, sound booms, and prompter, each with their own operators. The output of cameras and mikes is transmitted via cables connecting to the fourth wall of the studio and thence to the gallery. People working on the floor will include the floor manager plus any assistants, camera operators, sound assistants and sparks. Dedicated studio cameras are mounted on gas-filled pedestals which means they can elevate and depress as well as pan and tilt. With built-in rubberised castors they can be tracked easily and silently anywhere along the studio floor.

The Gallery

Seated in the production gallery are the director, the production assistant, the vision mixer and the technical manager. The producer will also probably be in the production gallery but seated back from the others. Sound and vision supervisors will be in their own galleries. Tape operators controlling play-in or record machines (**VTs**) will be wherever their machines are located. This may be in the production gallery or in a VT bay somewhere else deep in the building wired to the gallery.

The director, production assistant and vision mixer sit at a console into which is built a mixer and effects bank. In front of them is a bank of monitors, each of which is showing the output of the various sources: each of the cameras, VTs, graphics, caption generator, remote studios, etc.

Two of the monitors – usually on top of the rest – show the **transmission (TX)** picture and the **preview** image. The TX picture is the source that the vision mixer has selected as the transmission picture at a given moment. The preview monitor shows the picture the vision mixer expects to be going to next. If there are separate control rooms, each will have its own set of monitors, replicating the set-up in the production gallery. The sound console will have a built-in sound mixer desk and machines for playing in music or sound effects. The lighting gallery will contain faders for the lights being used and controls for monitoring and controlling picture quality – referred to as **racks**.

Selecting Output

In the production gallery the vision mixer selects the transmission output by pressing an illuminated, numbered button on the mixer. The first numbers from 1 upward will correspond to the individual numbers of each of the cameras. Other sources are then allocated the remaining higher numbers. So, for example, if you were working with four cameras, two VT machines and a remote studio the mixer numbers could be allocated as follows:

SOURCE	MIXER No
Camera 1	1
Camera 2	2
Camera 3	3
Camera 4	4
VT1	5
VT2	6
New York Studio	7

The vision mixer's **effects bank** controls the look of the transition from one transmission picture to the next. With nothing selected a straight cut results but there is usually the option to use dissolves (or mixes) and wipes. The more sophisticated the set-up, the more varied and complex the mixing options. The range of visual effects possible in a studio are very similar to those used in an online edit suite and are explored in more detail in Chapter 16. In some studios – particularly where there is heavy use of chromakey – it is not uncommon for two vision mixers to work alongside one another managing the effects.

The last point to realise about the physical set up of most studios is that people working in the galleries cannot see through to the studio floor. All they see is the studio's output – what the cameras are seeing. This might seem to be an impossible way to work. In fact it is far better to concentrate solely on the output of monitors. But you do need to have a good mental picture of where cameras are, whether they are getting caught up in one another's cables, likely to bump into one another or appear in one another's shots.

Communication

When a well rehearsed and fully prepared production is actually being transmitted or recorded, the only people who should be talking will be the director, the production assistant and the vision mixer. These three communicate with the entire team through a system known as **talkback**. A mike on the gallery desk picks up everything they say – open or omni talkback (from omnibus – for everyone). Their instructions are then relayed to the other control rooms, the VT bay and anyone on the floor wearing **cans** or headphones. This would normally only be the floor manager, camera operators, teleprompt and sound boom operator. Anyone else on the floor would follow voice or hand signals from the floor manager. The director's open talkback is usually only one way – from the director to everyone else.

Anyone needing to talk to the director would use **switch talkback**. Before talking – usually only when asked to do so by the director during rehearsal – they would flick or hold down a switch to do so. The reason for talkback being open only one-way is fairly obvious. The director doesn't want to be listening to a host of disembodied voices chatting to one another as they sort out their particular problems. This is quite apart from the need to spare the director the embarrassment of overhearing technicians taking bets on whether this production is going to turn out to be as big a shambles as the last fiasco they worked on. The director might also have a separate switch talkback facility into the presenter's ear. Cameras also communicate visually with the director. On rehearsal if a camera operator wants to come onto talkback to the director the convention is for the camera to keep zooming in and out until the director says 'Yes, Pete, talk to me'. The director should have a list of the names of the camera operators and their camera number in front of him and try to talk to them as human beings rather than by number. Cameras respond to a question from the director by either tilting up and down – nodding Yes – or panning back and forth from left and right – No.

Cabling Cameras

If you are directing a studio shoot one of the first questions you will need to answer is – how do you want the cameras to be cabled? In the gallery the monitors will be showing you the camera's output in number order from left to right.

Let's say you are going to be shooting a discussion between two people – one either side of the presenter.

Assuming you have three cameras facing the set, to get decent eyelines the two outside cameras will be cross-shooting. The left-hand camera will be shooting the person camera right and the right-hand camera will be shooting the person camera left. If you cable the cameras from left to right going 1 2 3, this is what you will see on the monitors.

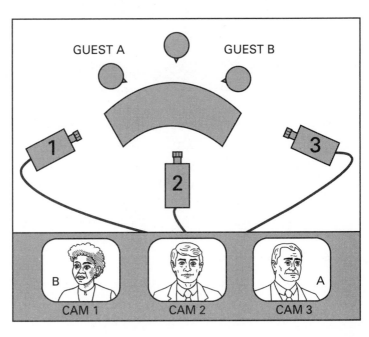

As you look at the monitors each of the two guests is facing out. This doesn't matter. When you cut between them it will look fine as far as the viewer is concerned. But it is a confusing set of images to work with so you would do much better to cable the cameras in reverse order 3 2 1.

That way this is what you will see on the monitors.

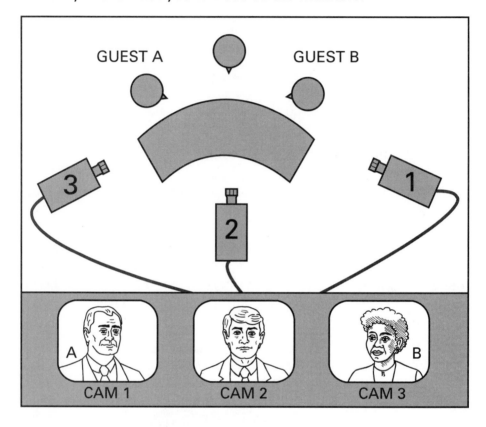

If you are using a prompt system you will also need to think about which camera or cameras it will be mounted on. There are two considerations here. You need to work out which cameras will be closest to your presenters. You then need to remember that with a prompt system mounted a camera is slightly less manouverable than normal. So don't expect the prompt camera to be able to tilt down much or to be able to get close ups of props on a low table.

The Process

As you can see, a studio shoot involves a large number of people and equipment. It won't happen unless there is a good deal of planning and communication. The planning process needs to start as early as possible and all communication needs to be as precise and detailed as possible. The planning process can be divided into the following stages:

- **Deciding Content.** At an early stage the producer – or whoever is responsible for the editorial content of a program – should discuss with the director what they plan to do and what they think they will need. If they are saying they want five separate discussion areas in a studio the size of the shoe box it is up to the director to say it can't be done or they will need to use a larger studio.

- **Deciding the Look.** Once the director knows what the editorial brief is a set designer will be briefed. Both producer and director might discuss their ideas with the set designer.

- **Technical Briefing.** The director should meet with the technical manager, the sound supervisor and the lighting supervisor and brief them on what it is anticipated will be needed. The set designer should also be at this meeting.

- **Set and Light.** The set is built or assembled in the studio and the lighting crew light it following the director's brief.

- **Camera Rehearsal.** The director and all of the technical crew 'stagger through' the program. Cameras are operated with shots and moves being rehearsed but the people who will be appearing on camera are probably not present. Lighting adjustments can be made based on what the cameras are actually seeing and showing and Sound can check that they have got mikes that work wherever they are needed. At this stage there could possibly be a script but there may only be a running order – a listing of the key sequences in the program and what happens in each of them.

- **Full Rehearsal.** This involves everybody and is more for those appearing on camera than for the technical crew who already know what they have to do. It is also an opportunity for Lighting to see the people who will actually be appearing and for Sound to listen to them. If presenters are using a prompt system they should deliver their pieces to camera using it and check it is how they want it. It is also an opportunity to check the link into any graphics or VT sequences that are going to be played into the program.

- **Record or Transmission.**

Paperwork

The type of paperwork that is needed, or that you will be able to produce, will vary depending on the kind of program you are shooting. We will work through a simple example.

Example

Your program consists of a title sequence, followed by a presenter, ZENA, to camera shot against Chromakey blue. ZENA introduces the first item, we cut away to a couple of graphics. She then links into a 2-minute VT package. We come back to her and she links into a discussion chaired by a second presenter, JOHN. At the end of the discussion ZENA pays off to camera and we end with closing titles from VT with the end credits being added from a caption generator. We will also be using the caption generator to superimpose name captions for each of the guests, Mr JONES and Mrs SMITH.

Running Order

The first thing to do is to draw up a running order. As it name suggests a running order is a sequentially numbered list of the elements that go to make up a program along with the duration of each sequence and the technical information that everyone needs to know for each one. Different programs may design their running orders to suit their particular needs. In this case the running order will start off looking like this:

SEQUENCE	POSITION	SOURCE	DUR
1	Opening titles	VT	00.30
2	ZENA to camera linking to	PromptCam + CSO	0.20
3	HOUSING PACKAGE	VT	02.03
4	ZENA to camera linking to	PromptCam + CSO	00.10
5	JOHN + 2 discussion	Cams	04.30
6	ZENA pay off	PromptCam + CSO	00.15
7	CLOSING TITLES	VT + CAPGEN	00.20

At this stage the running order is incomplete. It only contains editorial information and an indication of the technical sources. The director now adds the rest of the information.

Floor Plan

Working with a floor plan of the studio, the director works out which cameras will be involved in each sequence and roughly what they will be doing. The floor plan of the studio is a bird's eye view showing where the cycle starts and finishes, all of the cable runs and the shootable floor area which will be painted and lit. In this case it also shows the position of the set – the desks or any other furniture that has already been decided on by the director and the designer. The set may be split up into a number of different areas – discussion desk, presenter in front of chromakey screen, etc.

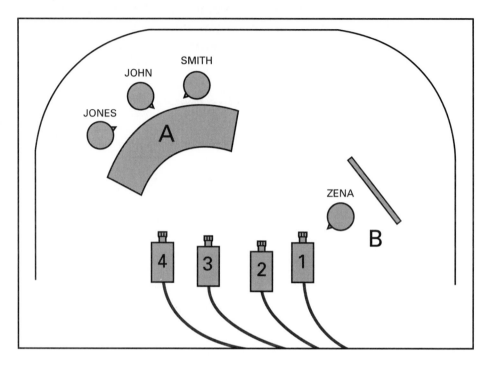

Each of these areas is designated by a letter; in this case A for the discussion desk, B for the presenter position.

We have four cameras cabled 4 3 2 1. The discussion area A is upstage left and the single presenter area B with a chromakey screen is downstage right. Only ZENA needs a prompt camera so you are going to have decide which it should be.

You also decide that at the end of Sequence 4 as ZENA links to the discussion you want to cut to a wide shot showing her in the foreground and the discussion area in the background.

Plotting Moves and Shots

Before you finalise the prompter decision you need to work out what shots you are likely to want and what each of the cameras will be doing. This can be a bit of a chess game. At the moment it looks as though Camera 1 would be the best choice for the prompter – but it's not that simple.

What you need to do is work out where you want cameras to be for the majority of the shoot and take account of what is likely to be happening when they make their first move. So you need to think ahead to the moment ZENA hands over to JOHN in the discussion area. You will want a camera on her, a camera to give you the linking shot showing her and the discussion area, a camera on JOHN and the two guests and a camera giving a single of the first guest he will be introducing. You also know that as soon as you cut to the linking shot, ZENA's camera goes to join the discussion, followed by the linking shot camera once you are off it.

Here is a solution:

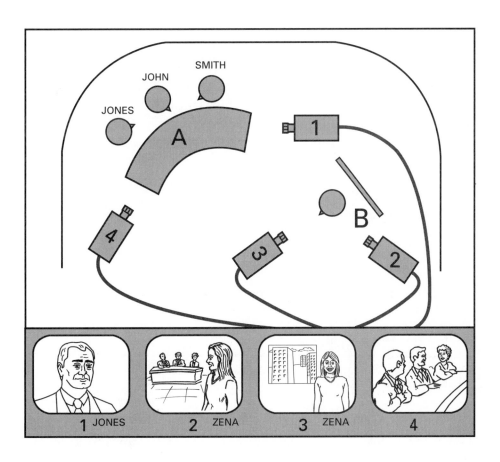

MULTI-CAMERA SHOOTS

The best shot of the person sitting camera left, Mr JONES, will be on Camera 1 and the best shot of the person sitting camera right, Mrs SMITH, will be on Camera 4. JOHN is going to introduce Mr JONES first. So Camera 1 will need to be offering Mr JONES' medium close up.

Camera 3 is ZENA'S camera on which you will mount the prompter, while Camera 2 gives the shot linking ZENA to Area A.

That leaves Camera 4 giving a 3-shot of JONES, JOHN and SMITH which you will be cutting to immediately after the handover shot on Camera 2 as JOHN introduces the discussion. You will then be going to Camera 1 as he tells us who JONES is and while you are on 1, Camera 4 will quickly zoom in on SMITH. You will then cut to 4 as JOHN says who SMITH is.

(Note that Camera 1 has gone right round the outside of the studio with its cable behind the CSO flat to take up position. This way there is no risk of the cable appearing in Camera 2's wide shot.)

Once they have finished on ZENA Cameras 3 and 2 will clear to join the discussion. They will be able to offer a variety of wide shots, singles of JOHN and alternative singles of SMITH and JONES. But they won't be able to offer such good eyelines as Cameras 4 and 1.

This is what will happen:

MS ZENA to camera   Camera 3

Link Shot ZENA   Camera 2   (Clear Cam 3 to Area A)
plus Area A

3-shot Area A as JOHN
introduces discussion   Camera 4   (Clear Cam 2 to Area A)

MCU JONES as   Camera 1   (Cam 4 zooms into
JOHN introduces him   MCU SMITH)

MCU SMITH as JOHN
introduces her   Camera 4

Detailed Running Order

You can now make up a more detailed running order:

SEQUENCE		POSITION	SOURCE	DUR
1	Opening titles		VT1	00.30
2	ZENA to camera plus graphics linking to	B	PromptCam 3 + CSO + FRAMESTORE	00.20
3	HOUSING PACKAGE		VT2	02.03
4	ZENA to camera Link shot Area B to Area A	B	PromptCam 3 + CSO Cam 2	00.10
5	JOHN intro Intro JONES Intro SMITH Discussion JONES, JOHN, SMITH	A	Cam 4 WA Cam 1 MCU JONES Cam 4 MCU SMITH Cams 1, 2, 3, 4 + CAPGEN	04.30
6	ZENA to camera pay off	B	PromptCam 3 + CSO	00.15
7	CLOSING TITLES		VT1 + CAPGEN	00.20

As well as thinking about what shots the cameras will be offering, the director has also had to consider how the VT packages are to be played in. If there are a number of different packages and not a lot of studio time between them, it is best to have them playing in from alternate machines. As you can see above VT1 has the opening titles, VT2 has the housing package and then it's back to VT1 at the end for the closing titles.

Camera Cards

The information on the running order can now be transferred to camera cards for each of the camera operators. So Camera 3's card will show:

Sequence 2	B	MS ZENA
Sequence 4	B	MS ZENA
Sequence 5	A	DISCUSSION WA & MCU JONES
Sequence 6	B	MS ZENA PAY-OFF

Camera cards are either produced in the production office and given to cameras or the camera operators may write them up themselves on the camera rehearsal. Operators will almost always add their own notes to prepared cards. For example towards the end of Sequence 5 Camera 3 will have to get from Area A back to ZENA in Area B. On rehearsal camera operator and director may agree this is going to take 10 seconds. The director won't actually give the operator a cue to move. They agree that the operator will take a cue from the production assistant's countdown – when the operator hears there is 15 seconds to go on the discussion. So the operator might just pencil *move on 15"* beside Sequence 5.

Script

The layout of a studio script follows the same principle as the shooting script for a single camera production shot on location. It is set out in two columns with visuals on the left and sound on the right. Each sequence is numbered, following the running order, and each shot is numbered. Because the program is being shot 'as live' each cutting point is clearly marked. The script also shows the duration of VT inserts and the IN and OUT words.

This is how the first part of the script for our worked example might look:

SEQUENCE 1 – TITLES

1	VT1 _____/	TITLES VT
		SOVT
		IN: MUSIC
		OUT: MUSIC STING
		DUR: 00.20

SEQUENCE 2 – HOUSING INTRO

2	CAM 3 ZENA + CSO_____/	ZENA:
		Hello and welcome.
		Tonight we report on the
		scandal of the city's
		housing policy.
3	GRAPHIC 1 _____/	This is how spending on
		homes for the city's
		poor has been cut over
		the past two years.
		Meanwhile
4	GRAPHIC 2 _____/	this is how taxes have
		been rising.
5	CAM 3 ZENA + CSO _____/	And as we found out,
		people who have to
		live in the council's
		properties are not at all
		happy. Rafiq Hussein
		reports.

SEQUENCE 3 – HOUSING VT

6	VT2 _____/	HOUSING VT
		SOVT
		IN: 'Talk to anyone who
		lives . . .
		OUT: . . . a lot of
		unanswered questions.'
		DUR: 03.20

SEQUENCE 4 – LINK TO DISCUSSION

7	CAM 3 ZENA + CSO _____/	ZENA:
		Well let's see if we can
		get some answers to
		those questions now.
8	CAM 2 _____/	John.

As you can see a line with a forward slash (____/) is typed across the page to show the exact cutting point for each shot. SOVT stands for sound on VT. If you were running film into a program it would come from a telecine machine, abbreviated to TC or TK. Nowadays this is unlikely as film is always transferred to VT before transmission. Graphics are usually created on **Paintbox** or a similar system and then stored for play-in on a magnetic disk called **Framestore**.

The full script will be needed by the presenters, producer, director, production assistant, vision mixer, technical manager, sound supervisor, lighting director, prompt operator and floor manager. Everyone else works off either the running order or camera cards.

Making It Happen

On full rehearsal or record/transmission the voice that everyone is listening to is that of production assistant (PA). It is the PA's job to call the shots and let everyone know where they are in the program and what's going to happen next. The PA is also responsible for timings and keeps stopwatches running on the overall program duration and on individual items. On a complex production there will often be two PA's – one calling the shots and the other monitoring timings.

The PA or the director will cue VT to run. Either the director or the vision mixer will cue cameras on shots that are required – but it's best if they decide beforehand which of them is going to do the talking. On a tightly-scripted production – say a drama – everything will be fully rehearsed. The PA calls the shots, the vision mixer talks to cameras if need be. The director is concentrating on the actors' performances and at the end of a take communicates with the performers through the floor manager. On a live magazine program or chat show the director will tend to do all the talking to cameras.

In our example this is the sort of dialogue that everyone could expect to hear on talkback as we come out of Sequence 3 and into Sequence 4:

PA: *Thirty seconds left on VT. Sequence 4 next.*

             Counting out of VT 10, 9, 8 . . .

             . . . 4, 3, 2, 1

             (Vision Mixer mixes from VT2 to Camera 3)

Director: *Cue ZENA . . . Coming to 2. On 2 . . . and . . . 4.*
             Coming to 1 . . .1. Clear 2 and 3. Steady 4. And 4.

This is often accompanied by a good deal of arm waving and conducting. Between them the camera operators and the vision mixer normally manage to make it all work despite the director.

That's what is happening in the gallery. Meanwhile on the studio floor the floor manager gives ZENA a countdown by holding up a hand with five fingers extended, dropping each one by the second, and then letting the hand fall just below the lens. At the same time a red cue light on top of the camera immediately illuminates as the vision mixer selects Camera 3 as the TX picture. ZENA knows she is on camera and flashes that smile she is famous for.

Shooting a Discussion

Once a program gets into an unscripted sequence such as a discussion the director has to start doing some serious work. You may have some idea of the order in which people are going to speak but the guiding principle is that you must be ready for anything to happen. The easiest way to ensure this is to always have one camera on a wide shot. But don't just keep one camera on the same old wide shot throughout. It's boring.

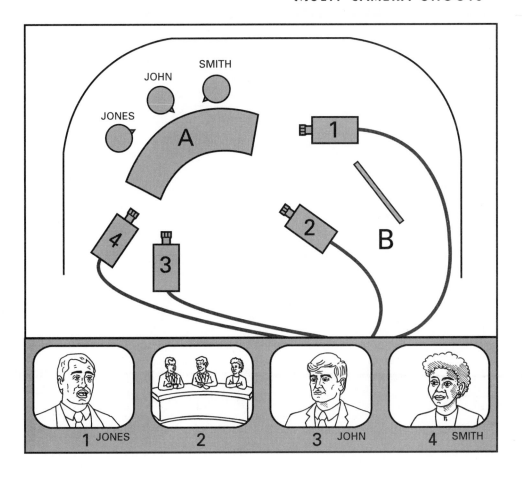

So let's say in our worked example you are on Camera 1 (the TX picture) with an MCU of JONES, Camera 2 is giving you a wide shot of the group, Camera 3 is on an MCU of JOHN who is looking toward the speaker, JONES, and Camera 4 is on an MCU of SMITH.

If JOHN looks as though he is going to put another question to JONES you might go to 3 to take it. But if he turns to bring in SMITH you have the option of going via the wide shot on 2 and then cutting to SMITH on 4.

This is what he does so you are now on Camera 4 showing SMITH.

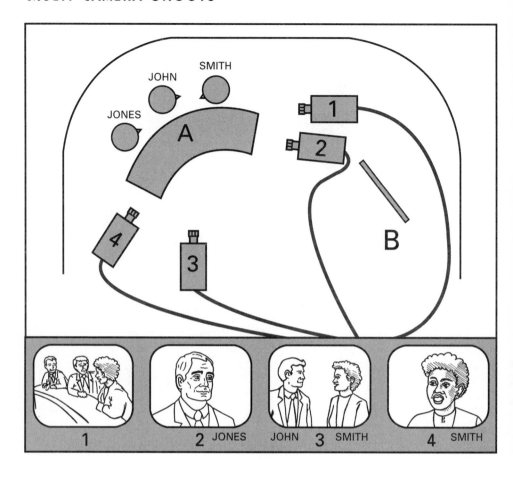

You get 1 to give you a 3-shot over SMITH's shoulder. But if JONES interrupts, or you want a reaction shot from him, you don't have a close shot so Camera 2 moves upstage and offers an MCU of JONES. Camera 3's single of JOHN isn't a lot of use now as he is turned away from camera so Camera 3 zooms out to give a 2-shot of JOHN and SMITH.

You cut to 3 as JOHN puts another question to SMITH but she is half way through her answer when JONES interrupts. You cut to 1's 3-shot favouring JONES and then pick him up on his single on 2. The eyeline isn't good.

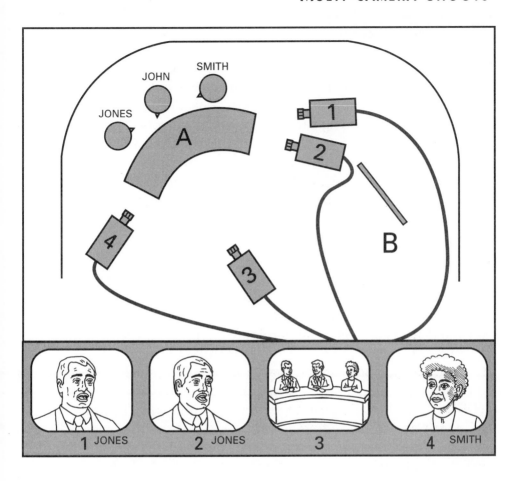

Camera 1 zooms into the better MCU on JONES. You can't cut from 2 to 1 – the shots are too similar. So Camera 3 moves swiftly downstage and comes out to a 3-shot. You cut to 3 for a couple of seconds and then to 1. Camera 2 could now come out wider to either a 2-shot of JONES and JOHN or a 3-shot; alternatively you could get Camera 2 to come downstage to offer a head on shot of the group while Camera 3 moves back upstage to give a close shot of JOHN looking towards JONES. And so it goes on . . .

Look and Listen

Directing any unscripted multi-camera sequence doesn't just involve making sure you have the right shots available and the right people covered by the cameras. It also involves looking and listening; listening to what is being said and looking at what is happening on all the cameras – not just the one currently selected. If SMITH is speaking and you are on her and she refers to something JONES has said, you need to see how JONES is reacting and then possibly cut back to him as he smiles, frowns, smirks or whatever.

Cues and Countdowns

During the discussion JOHN needs to know how long he has got to go, when he should wind it up and when he should hand back to ZENA. The producer will have allotted a specific period of time for the discussion – let's say 5 minutes. If this is a live program, it's important JOHN sticks to this or it could throw out the timings for the entire show. Every minute the PA will call out the number of minutes to go – '4 minutes to go on discussion'. If JOHN is wearing an earpiece he will hear this on switch talkback. If he isn't he will be getting visual cues. The floor manager will be positioned somewhere out of shot but in JOHN's eyeline and will hold up a hand with four fingers extended. At three minutes he will hold up three fingers and so on. With 10 seconds to go the floor manager holds up both hands with all fingers and thumbs extended and if JOHN starts to overrun the floor manager then makes a cutting gesture across the throat.

If the overall timing is not too critical and the producer wants to bring the discussion to a gentle conclusion – usually because the guests are agreeing with one another and the viewers are starting to switch channels – the floor manager will wind an arm in slow circles – a slow wind. If the guests still keep chatting on and JOHN hasn't quite got the message the floor manager will give him a fast wind. Alternatively, if the discussion is going particularly well and the producer decides to let it run beyond the planned duration, the floor manager gives a 'stretch' signal placing the palms of both hands together and then stretching them apart.

The decision to wind early or to stretch is an editorial decision taken by the producer who then communicates it via the director and PA to JOHN. They both need to know the decision – it may mean a change of plan from what was rehearsed – and they are the ones who then need to relay it to the floor. A third voice no one has heard before suddenly coming on talkback is a recipe for confusion.

Outside Broadcasts

The set-up for a multi-camera outside broadcast is very similar to the one we have seen in the studio. The difference is that instead of a gallery, the production team work from a mobile scanner. The scanner contains a scaled down mixer desk built into a van or truck. A full-scale OB unit could consist of four or five vehicles – the scanner truck, sound, a mobile control room, a generator truck, etc. As well as many of the people we have encountered in the studio an OB unit will also need riggers, engineers and drivers. There's not a lot of room in a scanner and very often directors will do their own vision mixing. One other difference is that the floor manager role on an OB is called the stage manager.

Again, you don't just book an OB unit and turn up at an event expecting it all to happen. A good deal of preparation is necessary. The first thing the director has to do is find out what is likely to happen during the event itself and then decide where cameras ought to be positioned. Will the camera positions allow you to cover all of the action from as many different angles as possible and – our old friend again – is there any danger of crossing the line? Get the answers to those two questions right and you are half way home.

Always try and get one camera at least shooting from as high an angle as possible. This will give a perspective that the viewers would not normally get themselves if they were spectators at the event. It will also give you the best master shot and help you out of any line crossing problems. But don't rely on a high angle camera to be able to offer very tight shots. As soon as the camera is in tight the slightest ground tremor will produce a very shaky picture.

Looking and listening is just as important on an OB as it is in the studio. Most outside broadcasts consist of live pictures with live on the spot commentary. Both need to work together. The commentator will have one eye on the event itself and the other on a monitor showing the TX picture. Most of the time the commentator will follow what is on the monitor but if something else is happening and the commentator mentions it, the director should try and get a camera on it and show it. There is nothing more frustrating for the viewers than hearing a commentator say 'Amazing scenes at the other end of the pitch as the police baton charge the English fans' while the pictures are showing yet another dismal game of football.

Chapter 13
Graphics, Titles and Rostrum Cameras

Graphics

Most programs contain graphics of some kind. These may be complex animations or they may be simply **name supers** or **captions** superimposed over a talking head to identify them and their role, position or function. There is an important principle to understand for any graphics containing text.

Title Safe

We've already seen how you have to allow for domestic cut-off when framing a shot. This applies even more when you are designing graphics and positioning name supers. Most graphics and edit monitors have a switchable grid that can appear on the screen to show you what is known as the **title safe area**. It looks something like this:

Text that is going to appear on the screen should be placed within the title safe area. If it isn't and you just guess at the positioning, there is a real risk of text appearing either right at the edge of a domestic monitor or starting to disappear off it. If you are getting graphics made up by a professional graphics designer, you shouldn't need to worry about this. It is something they check as a matter of course. But it is still worth making sure.

The problem is more likely to occur if you are working with a designer with a print or computer slides background. They are used to working in a 'what you see is what you get' environment and will need to be made aware of the title safe problem. Similarly, if you are using a PC or Mac to design graphics yourself make sure you keep text well within the screen.

When you are shooting a talking head you also need to allow enough room in the lower third of the screen for the person's name super to appear later.

If you have shot an entire interview in a tight close up, the name super is going to run right across the subject's mouth.

Captions

The standard way of creating captions electronically is to use a **caption generator** when you come to online edit your program. These come under a variety of manufacturer's names, the best known of which is Aston. Less well known, but in fact more versatile, is Collage. Creating a caption is relatively simple. You type in the characters you want on a dedicated keyboard and they appear on the monitor as white lettering on a black background. If you want to, you can then colour them up and arrange the text on the screen wherever you want it. A variety of different fonts or typefaces is available. Captions can be static or they can roll or scroll. Rolling means they travel up or down the screen and disappear off it – end credits for example. Scrolling – also referred to as crawling – means they travel horizontally across the screen – coming in from the right and going off on the left.

Most caption generators allow you to store all your text captions so that they can be called up as and when required, either on a multi-camera shoot or an online edit. You may also be able to type up all your text on a PC and give the Capgen operator or your editor all the data on a floppy disk. This can save a lot of keying-in time in the edit and minimises the risk of spelling mistakes. But check first what file format the caption generator can read. It will usually need to be an ASCII file. Always proof-read the text on screen for spelling mistakes.

So you have got a name super made up. How do you add it to the live action shot of someone speaking? The answer is you use a **matte**.

Mattes

A matte consists of two areas of an image – one coloured solid white and the other coloured solid black. A white text caption on black is a matte. This image A is keyed with another image B – a talking head. The black area of A is the 'fill'. The black area on A fills with the picture on B. What you see is the talking head with the text caption apparently superimposed.

In this case you are keying off black. You can also key off white. If you generated the caption in black on a white background and selected the white key you would get a black text caption superimposed on the talking head.

You can use mattes to combine a graphic with live action. Say you want to show a map of the United States and then have live action appear within its borders, while still seeing the rest of the map – part of Canada and Mexico. You – or your graphics designer – creates the full map as a graphic and saves it. You could then colour the United States white and the rest of the picture black. This is your matte. When you edit you can combine the graphic, the matte and a live action shot to achieve the effect. The graphic is keying off black and the live action is keying off white.

Graphic Map

Here are the three images you are working with:

Matte of United States

Live action shot of truck

By using matte keys and combining all three images, this is what you could end up with:

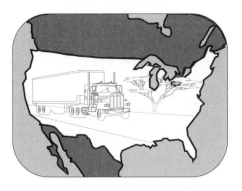

The graphic map and the matte would be created in a
paint program.

It is of course vital that the map graphic and its matte are
in register. They must both be exactly the same size and in
exactly the same position on the screen.

The graphics would be married up with the live action in the
online edit.

Whenever you are getting graphics made up, particularly if you
are using company logos, it is advisable to get mattes made at
the same time. They don't take long to do and they will always
give you more options when you edit.

Choosing a Graphics Designer

Television graphic designers work with a variety of computer
systems and software. The best known of these is Paintbox –
another proprietary name that has become generic. Paintbox is a
grown up version of the Paint program that comes bundled with
most PCs. The big difference is that it is designed specifically for
television graphics. However, as the power of PCs and Macs has
increased, more and more designers are finding that they can
achieve just as good results with much cheaper programs such as
Photoshop running on standard PCs and Macs.

Which should you go for? There is no easy answer. A lot will
depend on how complex you want your graphics to be and how
much money you have to spend. But what matters far more is the
person. A good graphics designer will know how to make their
particular system work to achieve what you want. They will also
tell you what you can do and what you can't do. And make sure
whoever is creating your graphics is a designer rather than just
an operator. There are a lot of operators around who know how
to drive the computer. This doesn't always mean they have a lot
of imagination or artistic ability.

As we have just seen with the example of mattes, graphics often
have to work with editing effects to achieve the result you are after.

In an ideal world your designer and editor should work with one another to make sure the designer is supplying all the elements that are required. In the real world this is seldom practical. So it's important your designer is someone who knows what can and cannot be done in the edit. Many edit suites offer graphics as part of the facility. Don't assume this means that the graphics department and the editors talk to one another. It is up to the producer or the director to make sure that what one has done will work with what the other is going to do. One way of making sure of this is to sub-contract a complex graphic sequence to a designer who effectively becomes the director responsible for the sequence and delivers it as a completed insert to the program.

The Process

Roughs

Rough out on paper the data that you want your graphics to contain. This will give you an idea of whether they are going to work visually. Designers work better from a visual brief than from a script, though they will need that too.

Briefing

Talk through the brief with the designer and suggest ideas for the look you are after. Unless you are a design whizz yourself, show the designer what you have got – a logo, selected live action shots, etc. and ask the designer to come up with an idea rather than dictate something.

Costing

Designers normally charge by the hour. Some work faster than others. It is best to show the designer the brief and then get a price for the whole job. How long it takes is then up to the designer.

Watching a designer at work is quite interesting for the first ten minutes. You get to see what the system is capable of. It is much better to give the brief, discuss and agree it, and then go away and let the designer get on with it.

You will usually need to come back to check the overall look before data is added. If you don't see the graphics until they are completed and then want to change the overall look, they may all need to be unstitched so that you can change a background colour. This can be expensive.

Once you have signed off on the graphics the designer saves them onto tape or disk.

A Few Design Principles

- The key to good design is simplicity. If a graphic isn't simple, it won't communicate. So keep text to a minimum. Any graphic containing text needs to stay on the screen long enough to be read by the viewer. If a graphic has to stay on the screen for any length of time it is going to slow down the pace of your program.

- Avoid use of strong colours – particularly primary red. If your program is going to end up being shown on VHS, red will be 'noisy'.

- Avoid flowery fonts for text – *this sort of thing may not work.* 𝔑𝔬𝔯 𝔪𝔞𝔶 𝔱𝔥𝔦𝔰.

  They are not easy to read and there is a danger that characters could break up. Most of the time you will want to use the bold version of a standard font such as Times, Helvetica or their equivalents. Anything with thin vertical lines could present problems.

- Think about the live shots name supers will appear over. If your name supers are all in white text and half the people in your program are wearing light clothing, the supers will be difficult to read. A good way round this is to have the supers appearing in a transparent band across the screen.

- If you are creating a series of graphics where data is going to build, create the final graphic first and then delete the build elements in reverse order, saving each one as a separate frame.

- Check and double-check all spelling.

- Check and double-check all figures.

Creating Your Own Graphics

If you are on a tight budget and your graphic requirements are fairly simple, there are two ways you can create your own graphics.

On a PC or Mac

If you have a PC with software for creating presentation slides you should be able to create acceptable graphics yourself and save them to disk in a format that your online edit suite can read. You may also need a good paint or draw program. But make sure the screen size or **aspect ratio** are the same on your saved image as they will be in the edit. Most presentation software works to a 35mm slide default which is slightly different from television. Graphics can take up a lot of memory. So you may need a Zip or Jaz drive – or a plentiful supply of floppy disks.

In the Edit

Alternatively, there are often ways you can create simple graphics in the online edit using a mixture of material you have shot and text from the caption generator. For example you could take a still frame from a live action sequence, **knock it back** – reduce normal luma and chroma levels – place a transparent panel over it and then arrange text on the panel.

Opening Titles

Almost every program needs an Opening Title. This could either be a graphic animation or a montage of fast cut live action shots to music. Or it could be something very simple – a company logo followed by a caption saying ANNUAL RESULTS.

Graphic animations are expensive and the cost is usually only justified if you are going to be using the opening title several times on a series of programs. In that case you will need something a bit special. An Opening Title wakes the viewers up to the fact that their favourite program is about to start and if the graphics are fancy enough the audience may even be persuaded that the rest of the program is going to be just as exciting.

If you decide you want to go the graphic animation route you will certainly need to employ the services of a graphics designer with access to a high-end computer graphics system.

Animation

The principle of animation will be familiar to most people. An animation consists of a series of drawn images which, when cut together, appear to form a continuous action. Animation can be either 2D or 3D. Two-dimensional animation (2D), is also known as flat animation.

An example of 2D animation would be a road appearing on a map. Some graphics software allows you to do this all in the graphics suite. If this isn't possible you would have to do it by creating mattes and then completing the job in the online edit.

3D animation gives a graphic a three-dimensional look. An object to be animated is drawn on the computer and then given a series of positions that it will move through. Once designer and director are happy with the way it looks on the computer it is then **rendered** frame by frame to tape. Depending on the complexity of the animation, this process can take a considerable amount of time and is often best done overnight.

If you want to produce cartoon-style animation you are probably best off getting a lot of the material hand-drawn and then transferring the artwork to computer. An experienced animator will suggest the best way of doing this. Static backgrounds and action are usually drawn separately and then keyed together. Dialogue can be added at the very end of the process or it can be recorded so that the animator draws lip movement to match it. By adding, transposing or chopping out frames in the edit you can often make voice and lip movement match more closely.

Rostrum Camera

If you are including **stills** – photographs or illustrations – in a program you will need to get them onto tape. To do this you will need to use a rostrum camera. Most edit and graphic suites usually include a Beta SP or Digibeta rostrum camera.

Basic set-up

The simplest rostrum camera set-up consists of a camera clamped so that it is pointing vertically downward. The camera's output is viewed on a monitor. It is pointing straight down at a lit table on which there is a sheet of clean glass. The image to be shot is then placed under the glass so that it stays perfectly flat. By adjusting the position of the image and the zoom lens on the camera you can frame the image as you want it. But with this type of set-up all you will get is a static image.

Motion control

If you want to move around on a still you will need to use a dedicated rostrum camera with motion control. Here what happens is that the camera is static but the table is motorised and is able to move in any direction on the horizontal plane. At the same time the camera can be programmed to zoom in or out. Let's say you had a still of a school photograph and you wanted to track along a line of faces and then zoom into the last one. The camera stays still, the table moves in the opposite direction to the way you want the tracking shot to appear and as it gets to the end of its move it stops and the camera gently zooms in. And guess what – it's all done by computer – plus a skilled operator and your good self.

Very often you may need to shoot transparencies or 35mm slides. Again, a rostrum camera will be needed. But make sure the rostrum camera you are using can handle them. And don't expect to be able to shoot more than a static of a 35mm slide. It is very unlikely you will be able to get in close enough to zoom.

Improvising

You can also improvise your own rostrum shoot. There is nothing to stop you sticking a still on the wall (Blu-Tack is best) and shooting it with your location camera. You can also shoot a still in the studio. But in both those instances you are unlikely to have the same degree of control over the shot that you can achieve on the rostrum.

Tip

If you are shooting a still this way, don't worry about sticking it up dead level. It's easier to adjust the camera so that it appears level.

Illustrations

If you are commissioning illustrations to include in a production always get the artist to give you plenty of spare picture round the edge of the illustration. You may want to zoom into a detail on the edge of the picture and if there isn't plenty of spare picture you may find yourself shooting off.

In this illustration the bag of money has been drawn too close to the edge. The camera won't be able to get a clean wide shot allowing for cutoff . . .

. . . and if you try and get a close up of the bag you will start to shoot off.

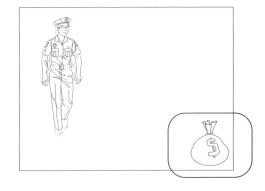

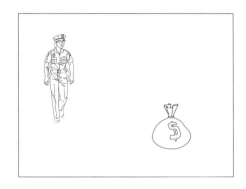

This is the way it should be – with the bag of money well into the illustration.

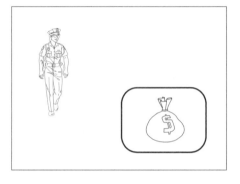

Now you can get a clean close up of the bag of money – and a clean wide shot. Illustrators expect the whole of their picture to be seen and sometimes have a little difficulty understanding the needs of the television producer. If you need to make the problem clear to them, show them this page and with a bit of luck you may get what you want.

CHAPTER 14
EDITING – TECHNICAL OVERVIEW

There are normally two stages to an edit – the offline and the online.

In the **offline** edit you view all your material and put the program together, perhaps making several versions of it until you are happy with the results. At this stage you will be working with a low quality copy of your rushes.

The **online** edit is your final assembly of the finished program. You will now be working with your original rushes, making any necessary adjustments to picture quality and creating a high quality edit master. It is also where you create and add any visual effects.

Offline Systems

There are two different systems you can use for offline – linear or digital. Although it is to some extent computerised, linear offline editing is a bit like trying to make up a printed document using a photocopier, scissors and paste. With digital or non-linear offline the whole process happens inside a computer and you cut and paste shots in just the same way as you would manipulate blocks of text on a wordprocessor.

Linear Offline

In a linear offline you will be working on tape with one or two play-in machines and one record machine. Each machine is linked to a monitor showing its output. The offline editor operates an edit controller to play and record, to shuttle back and forth and to mark edit IN and OUT points.

You work with either SHVS or Umatic copies of your rushes – **transfers**. If you are going to be using a linear system you will first have to get all your Beta SP rushes transferred to either Umatic or SVHS with burnt-in time code (BITC) also referred to as window-code. This is the hidden time code on your rushes. With

BITC the time code now appears on your transfers as a white on black panel in the bottom of your picture.

You need time code for several reasons:

- as a visual reference to find shots and to know where you are on the transfers

- so that the edit controller has information to work with

- so that in the online edit you are using exactly the same frames from your rushes to compile your finished program.

With linear editing you have to compile the program shot by shot. Once you have laid down two shots you cannot go back and insert a third shot between them. You have to record the new shot over what was previously your second shot and then relay that shot in its new position. If you have edited a twenty minute program and there are changes to be made you have to copy whole sections, make the change, copy a bit more, make another change, etc.

In a linear offline everything is happening in real time. Each time you record – or lay down – a shot you have to watch it through as it plays. You will probably have done this already a few times as you have previewed the edit before finally deciding it works and hitting the edit button.

Once you have completed your offline and you are ready to online it, you or your editor has to produce an edit decision list (EDL) for use by the online suite. An EDL consists of a list of the IN and OUT time codes for every shot in the program. Modern systems can generate an EDL automatically onto floppy disk but there are older ones around where you have to read all the codes off the screen and write them down manually. When we get to looking at what happens in an online suite, we'll see how an EDL is used.

Linear editing is time-consuming and restrictive. But it is the cheapest way of editing so you may find you have to do it. It does have one thing going for it. It forces you to make up your mind.

Digital Desktop Offline

Digital non-linear offline is a lot less painful. The best known systems are Avid, Lightworks and Media 100. They are basically very high performance desktop computer systems with massive storage disks. The great advantage they have over linear editing is their flexibility. You can trim, extend or insert shots without having to constantly copy and re-record sections of the program. Added to which when you insert a shot all you have to do is give the computer the IN and OUT codes. The insert is then immediately present in the program. You don't need to sit and watch it playing in.

The physical set-up is also a lot less cumbersome than that of a linear suite: the computer, usually two hard disk drives, a keyboard and two monitors. Monitors are normally set up so that you preview shots – or clips – on one and view the result of your editing decisions on the other.

A digital edit works like this. First, you **digitise** your rushes. You play them in off a Beta SP machine (or whatever machine is compatible with your rushes) and record them in digital format onto the computer at low resolution where they are stored on hard disk. As the rushes are being digitised the computer reads in and records the time code automatically. You can then view the digitised contents of each roll and break them down into separate clips. A clip could be a single frame or a whole series of shots. You give each clip a name and file it wherever and however you want it on the system. For example, you could create separate folders for each of your program sequences and put the shots you think you will need for each sequence into each of those folders.

When you start to edit you select the clip you think you are going to need, view it again, mark the precise IN and OUT points and drop it into the program. However, when you compile shots this way you are not in fact creating a physical program. You are creating a **timeline** which tells the computer what **media** – your sound and pictures – it needs to play off the hard disk at a given moment. The timeline can always be visible at the base of one of the monitors. It shows all the clips in the order they appear with their names and you edit the program by editing the timeline.

Inserting another shot is just a mouse click away.

All of the information the system needs – timeline, time codes, editing instructions, etc – is known as the **project**. Storing a project file on the system isn't usually a problem. If you want to come back a few days later and edit, it should still be there. It's also simple to copy and it may work on another system. But what is unlikely to be still on the hard disk is your media. It will be taking up a lot of hard disk space. Unless you have made special arrangements to store it – an additional cost – it will have been wiped and so your rushes will have to be redigitised. Rather than putting the whole lot back on, you could choose just to redigitise the clips that are actually used in the project.

Online Systems

There are three different ways you can online a program to produce an edit master:

- linear

- digital desktop

- digital tape.

Autoconform

With all three you will probably want to **autoconform** your program first. What you are doing is effectively rebuilding your program – but this time using your rushes to obtain the best quality sound and pictures. Autoconforming takes a lot of the tedium out of assembling an edit master – except for the unfortunate who has to do it.

On a **linear** or **digital tape** autoconform the EDL disk is fed into a computer linked to play machines and the record machine. The computer looks at the EDL and asks for Roll 1. The operator or editor then sticks Roll 1 of the rushes into a play machine. The play machine consults the EDL then searches for the IN and OUT time codes for the first clip from that roll. It then locks up with the record machine and they do the business together. Just to add to the magic, the record machine positions the clip exactly where it needs to be on the tape in the finished program. The play machine then searches for the next shot from Roll 1, the record machine looks to see where its tape needs to be and records. So it goes on. With Roll 1 done you move on to the next roll and so on. All the editor is doing at this stage is feeding rushes into the play machines – and trying to stay awake.

If your offline system is not set up to produce an EDL and you cannot autoconform the program, the online editor is going to have to do it the hard way. The simplest method is to record the offline master onto your online edit master tape and then paste up the rushes to it. The online editor keys in the IN and OUT time codes visible on your offline edit master and records each shot from the rushes onto the edit master. Alternatively, the offline editor writes up a manual log of every time code and the online editor keys each of them into the system and assembles the program shot by shot. Both these methods are extremely boring, tedious, error-prone and – compared with autoconform – expensive. You will save money by using an offline suite that can produce EDLs and that allows you to autoconform.

A point to note about time code: an online edit master has its own hidden time code starting at zero and going to however long the program is. There is no way you can examine an edit master to see where the shots have come from. If you need to do that you will have to go back to the offline log, the EDL, the project or the offline edit master if you have used rushes with their own burnt-in time code.

On a **digital desktop online** autoconforming is standard. Rushes are played in from a tape machine and the computer then records the shots it needs at high resolution onto its hard disk. In this case though it is the project file that is telling the computer what it needs. Where it puts the new media on the disk doesn't matter. The timeline will dictate what is played when.

A point to note about roll numbers. It doesn't matter what roll number you gave a tape when you were shooting. The roll numbers that will apply in an edit are those assigned to each tape by the offline editor. These are the numbers that will also be used in the online. And they are good old fashioned numbers scrawled in marker pen on gaffer tape and stuck to the cassettes and their boxes. They need not bear any relation to the time code on your rushes but they will appear on the EDL or project file.

Online Editing

Once a program has been assembled the online editor and the director go through it adding name supers and any visual effects that are required. They are also checking for picture quality. Colour and lighting levels can be adjusted within certain tolerances. In addition they should also be checking that the autoconform hasn't missed anything. They should also be looking for any 'dropout'. Individual frames may not have been perfectly recorded – either on the autoconform or the rushes. If the problem is on the rushes and not too many continuous frames are affected, some repair may be possible.

A **linear online edit** suffers from the same restrictions as a linear offline. You are tied to all the edits and shots you decided on in the offline. You could replace one particular shot with another but the new shot would have to be exactly the same length as the old one. You will also need to have accurately estimated the timing of any special effects – in the offline. You cannot trim, extend or insert shots without making another real-time copy of whole sections of the program. If this is what you are forced to do your edit master will be down a generation. Your first edit master is by definition second generation anyway (copied from the rushes). On Beta SP this is barely noticeable but if you start going down by too many generations quality will start to suffer. Linear online is relatively inexpensive but you will be paying the full hourly rate as you copy your program to make one small change. It can start to be a false economy.

With **digital online** – either desktop or tape – you don't suffer the same restrictions. You can make what adjustments you want without paying any time or quality penalties. But you will be paying top dollar if you opt for digital tape online editing. The hourly rates for digital desktop online tend to be roughly the same as for linear online but there's a catch. With linear online once you have set up and recorded a visual effect it is there on the tape. With digital desktop when you set it up to happen it looks fine and it happens. But when you come to run the whole program the computer says it needs to render all the effects before it can play the program continuously. And even something as simple as a name super counts as an effect. You just have to sit there and let it render – or push off to the pub for an hour.

Another slight drawback with digital desktop online is the quality issue. You have already digitised your rushes – albeit at high resolution. When you have completed the edit on the computer, you are going to have to play it back out to tape so that you have an edit master for either transmission or duplication. Some loss of quality is inevitable but unless you are a hypertechie it is not enough to lose any sleep over.

Visual Effects

Visual effects fall into two broad categories:

- 2D effects such as mixes and wipes which will be standard on most mixer desks

- 3D effects where a moving image is grabbed and can be moved about the screen.

On a **tape online** – either linear or digital – the complexity of the effects you want will determine how many play-in machines you need and how many effects channels you require. Effects channels are often referred to as **DVE** (digital video effect).

If all you are going to be doing is straight cuts, all you will need is one play-in machine and one record machine – plus probably a caption generator which should come as standard in the suite.

If you are going to be including mixes or other simple 2D effects, you will need two play-in machines and a record machine. In theory the number of effects channels you require depends on the number of effects happening simultaneously on the screen. This is sometimes referred to as the number of layers of pictures

– or **multi-layering**. If you wanted two pictures to come zooming out over the top of a third you would need three play-in machines and two channels of effects. One way round this is make up the effect in stages and 'dump' each stage back to tape and then play it in to add the next stage – but on a linear online this will result in some loss of picture quality. You are copying and recopying.

In some online edit suites one channel of effects will come as standard. In others you may pay extra by the hour. If you are having to pay extra, or think you will need a second or third channel and additional machines, there's no need to book them for the whole session. Get all the simple stuff out of the way first – quality check and captions – then start adding your effects.

On a **digital desktop online** you don't need to worry about play-in machines or effects channels. In theory there is no limit to the number of picture layers you can work with. 2D effects are standard, as is caption generation, and the system should have 3D effects attached – but check first. For what you will be paying, desktop online systems are extremely versatile but they don't key one image off another quite as cleanly as tape online systems and they do take time to render any visual effects.

Going Straight to Online

There is no reason, technically, why you need to do an offline edit before you do an online. If you are shooting in the morning and editing in the afternoon for transmission in the early evening you will probably go straight to online. The main reason for offline edits is cost. A top of the range online edit could be costing you almost as much per hour as an offline edit is costing per day. So if you are going straight to online – plan your shoot carefully, keep your shooting ratio as low as possible and be very clear in your mind what you want to do in the edit.

Chapter 15
Editing Techniques

Offline and Online Editors

Program making requires a lot of equipment and a lot of technology. But what makes the difference between a good program and an average one is people. This is particularly true in the case of offline and online editors. In most cases the roles are performed by two separate people who need never meet though sometimes an offline editor might help supervise an online. Otherwise the director is the link between them. With digital desktop editing, however, more people are tending to do both jobs.

An offline editor can become very involved with a program and in an ideal world is working with the director rather than simply carrying out a string of instructions. Unfortunately many directors and editors have grown up with linear editing where the director had to sit there saying 'Do this next' and the editor simply did it. Digital desktop offline means that the director is much more able to leave the editor to get on with it and then come back and discuss the work so far. A good offline editor will often have as good if not a better idea of how to construct a sequence than a director will. Directors can always make positive use of the experience and the contribution that a good editor brings to a production.

The contribution that online editors make is slightly different. By the time the program gets to them the overall structure is fixed. In terms of actual editing all that an online editor might suggest is tweaking an edit by a few frames to improve it. The online editor's real skills are in driving the equipment to create the visual effects the director wants. On occasion the director may not be very sure, or very clear, about what is wanted. Then the online editor might suggest a way of creating an interesting transition. Alternatively, the director might have a very ambitious idea which is beyond the capability of the equipment in that particular suite. A good online editor will help find a way round this.

The Offline Process

The offline editing process can be broken down into 7 key stages:

1   Director views material

2   Director does paper edit

3   Editor and director view material

4   Editor compiles program following paper edit

5   Director and editor review first cut

6   Editor does fine cut

7   Director and editor review fine cut and make final changes

In practice it doesn't always happen like this. Often there isn't time and it is quite possible to condense the process into one stage – director and editor slam it all together because there is only an hour to go before transmission. But let's imagine there is time to do it properly. This is what could happen.

Stage 1   All the rushes are transferred to VHS with BITC and the director views all the material in the comfort of home or office. This is an opportunity to see what has worked and what has not worked on the shoot, what will cut satisfactorily and what soundbites from interviews the director might want to use. As well as the VHS transfers, the director might also be working with typed transcripts of any interviews.

Stage 2   Once all the material has been reviewed, the director can decide whether the original structure of the shooting script still works. It may be that in the course of shooting the storyline has changed. The script may be need to be altered. Against the new script, the director lists the time codes of the shots that could be used for each sequence. This is the paper edit. If the offline is to be on a digital desktop system, it may only be necessary to digitise these particular shots – or 'clips'. In a digital offline you can organise all the clips into folders of your choice to assist the search and selection process.

Stage 3 Director and editor go through the editing script and view the material to be used. It is important that the editor has a good feel for the structure, style and pace of the program. The director may have been living with the program for the past few weeks. This is the probably the first time the editor has had anything to do with it.

Stage 4 The editor compiles the program. If the final commentary has not been recorded (usually the case) the director records a **scratch commentary** for the editor to work with. The editor now starts putting the program together following the paper edit. If this is a linear offline the director will almost certainly have to be present throughout. If it is a digital offline – and the schedule and budget are sufficiently generous – the director could leave the editor to get on with it.

Stage 5 Once the first **rough cut** is completed director and editor review it together. They will be looking at various aspects of the program – does it hang together, is the overall structure right, is it telling the story simply and clearly, do individual sequences work visually, do individual edits work satisfactorily or is there some material missing? (i.e. the director either forgot to shoot something or didn't shoot something properly). If the answer to any of these questions is No, they will have to work out what changes are necessary and what can be done to get round any of the problems identified.

Stage 6 With those decisions taken the editor completes the **fine cut** of the program.

Stage 7 The fine cut is reviewed and final changes made.

But that's not quite the end of the story. The producer will want to see it. So will the client. So be ready to defend your decisions – and then to back off and make the changes they want. Producers and clients almost always want to change something – they have to justify their existence and their salaries. So if you think you have made the best program in the world you could leave something in that you want them to change or take out. If they don't spot it, you may have to suggest it as a change. They may say 'No we like it, leave it in.' Not much you can do about that.

Do's and don'ts

In the chapters on shooting we have already touched on the key rules that govern editing – not crossing the line and maintaining continuity. There are few other do's and don'ts to be aware of:

☐ Don't hold individual shots for too long. If you do, you will slow down the pace and your program will be boring. If you are short of pictures, try and cut the commentary down rather than extending a shot beyond its natural life.

☐ Try and avoid using the same shot twice – unless it is for effect, say in a reprise at the end of a program.

☐ Allow voice-over commentary to breathe. It should not be wall-to-wall. At the end of a thought or paragraph allow a pause before cutting to another shot, pause again and then restart the commentary.

☐ When cutting out of someone speaking try and avoid cutting on an upbeat – or where it is obvious they were going to go on to say something else. It sounds as if you have cut them off in their prime.

☐ Try and avoid every interview soundbite starting with the word 'Well . . .'. It's the way people speak but it is irritating to listen to. Try and chop out 'wells'.

☐ Watch for continuity of body movement on action sequences. If a person has their left leg forward on the first shot are they still in step on the next shot? If they are not, it will look odd.

Getting Out of Trouble

We have seen earlier how you can cover yourself in the shoot if there is a risk of breaking the rules – giving the editor wide shots and cutaways to get out of trouble. If this sort of material has not been shot, or if material has been shot incorrectly, there may be ways in the edit that you can salvage your program and your reputation.

Example

You have shot an interviewee and a reporter both looking the same way and you need to use the reporter's cutaway question.

Flop one of the images so the person appears to be looking the other way – you may not be able to do this until the online so producer and client are going to see the mistake. And be warned, the person's hair will be parted on the wrong side (the presenter might sue). Any lettering in the background – signs, book titles etc – is going to be back to front.

Example

You need to chop out a phrase or sentence from an interview. You are on a talking head and you have nothing else to cut away to.

A straight picture cut will result in a **jump cut**. The person's face will suddenly shift in the frame at the edit point. One solution is to mix the picture at this point. It's obvious that something odd has happened but it is less ugly than a jump cut. Some directors are getting round this problem with a flash effect. Hopefully, this won't catch on.

> ## Example
>
> You have forgotten to shoot a vital shot in an action sequence. As a result you are going to have to put together two shots that mean you cross the line.

Again a slow mix between the two shots is probably the best solution. Half the audience will think it is what you meant to do all along and the critics will write it up as being amazingly meaningful and artistic. If you can't mix – because this only a two machine edit or the program style forbids it – tough.

> ## Example
>
> Despite your best efforts on the shoot a vital interview contains a string of Ums and Ers. The interviewee just couldn't do it but in amongst it all they are saying something important.

There is only one way round this. Edit the sound track and chop out all the hesitations. Your picture will be a mass of unusable jump cuts. Establish the interviewee for as long as it takes to add their name super and paste over the rest with any relevant or half-way relevant live action shots – wallpaper. If you didn't shoot any wallpaper, it's smacked wrists time. You knew at the time this interview would present an editing problem.

Shots that Will Cut

As a general rule you can cut from one shot to another so long as each of the shots is sufficiently **different**. Different means either the subject matter is different or, if the subject matter is the same, the size of shot or the angle from which each is shot is different. However, even if the shot size and/or angle of shooting are different, any action must appear to be continuous – there must not be a break in continuity. If the subject is the same, each shot must be a different view of the same continuous event.

For example if you had these two wide shots of the same scene you could not cut directly from one to the other. One is only slightly tighter than the other. They won't cut and if the director doesn't believe it, the editor will say so.

Condensing Action

Skilful editing allows you to condense action and make it happen on screen in less time than it would in reality. Think back to the example of the woman walking up the path to the house. Because you have got a sufficient variety of different sized shots from different angles you can make her get there in far less time than the whole action really takes to happen. If all you had shot was the master shot that's what you would be stuck with and there would be no way of shortening it.

Punctuation

When we write we use punctuation such as commas and full stops to indicate where one thought ends and another starts. You can do the same thing visually and with sound to mark the end of one sequence and the start of another. A wide shot at the end of a sequence is saying 'and so we say farewell' – car drives off down wide shot of road, couple walk off into sunset, etc. Starting a sequence with a close up with strong sync sound – phone ringing, electric drill, engine firing up, etc – can wake the viewers up and make them think 'hello we seem to be somewhere else now, what's going on here?'.

Split Edits

As well as cutting pictures you are also going to be making sound cuts. You don't have to just make straight cuts on both sound and picture at the same time. You can separate a picture from its sync sound and create a split edit.

Example

On an interview you could start off seeing a sync shot of the interviewee speaking and then on their final words cut to the reporter nodding. On the same shot the reporter then asks the next question.

The diagram below shows what is happening on this particular split edit:

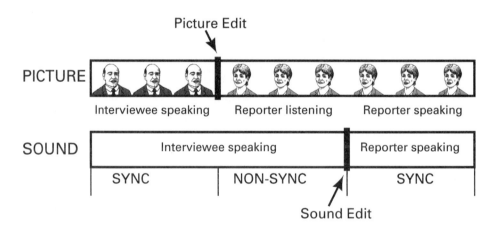

In other words the outgoing sync sound and the incoming picture overlap.

Cutting to Music

Using music can give a considerable lift to a program and create a mood or atmosphere that adds to the impact of your words and pictures. The trick is to use music effectively. A music sequence that works is one where the type of music matches the style of the pictures and where the pictures are cutting in time to the music. This may sound obvious but if you cut your pictures first and then try and add music, the effect won't be as good as if you lay down the music and then cut to it. That way you can cut on the beat of the music and also select shots that work with a particular passage of music at a given moment. If you have chosen music with a slow, lyrical theme it is likely to work best with slow, gentle pans or tracking shots. If the music has a fast beat you may want to cut a series of fast close ups to it. As the music builds to a crescendo, you might want your shots to become wider and wider. If the music contains all three elements and you have the shots to match you have got yourself a nice sequence.

It is always worth thinking about what music you may want to use before you even start to shoot. And if you know you are going to be cutting shots to music, shoot plenty of material. Don't worry too much about shooting ratios. If you have chosen the music before you shoot, play it to the camera operator so they have a feel for the type of shots you are after. Or you hum it, they shoot it.

Making it Fit

Very often you will want to make shots fit within the confines of a particular passage of commentary or music. There may be a particular shot you know you want to end with. Lay that shot down first in its position, backing it off from the end of the sound sequence. Then build the rest of the sequence in front of it. That way you know how much time you have got before the final shot and the number of shots you are likely to need.

Learning from the Edit

There is always something new you can learn from an edit. Everyone makes mistakes or wishes they had shot something differently. The secret is not to repeat the mistake and to get it right next time. Most editors are diplomatic souls and won't tell you that the material is utter rubbish but it is always worth a director asking an editor whether there was enough of the right material to work with.

Editing Techniques

You might get an answer such as 'Well, I could have done with the odd cutaway on such and such a sequence.' It's not the end of the world but it is useful information for next time.

However, any director who turns up with six hours of material to be edited down to three minutes in half a day, should not be surprised to be directed to the nearest watering hole while the editor attempts to salvage something from the wreckage.
Nor should the director expect to be viewing a masterpiece on their return.

Most editors work on a great variety of programs with a number of different directors. They get to see how it is done and how it should not be done in a range of different shooting set-ups. Directors can learn a lot by tapping an editor's experience. If a director is planning a shoot – and isn't quite sure the method is going to work – it's always a good idea to discuss it with the editor beforehand. They've seen it all.

Chapter 16
Online Editing

As we have already seen in Chapter 14, an online edit can be completed on a linear tape, a digital tape or a digital desktop system. An online edit is principally a picture edit. But if the soundtracks are relatively simple you can also mix your final soundtrack in the online as well. If they are at all complex, it is far better to mix the sound in a dubbing theatre after the online. Post-production sound is dealt with in the next chapter.

We have also covered the online process – assembling all the pictures in an autoconform using an EDL derived from the offline, checking picture quality and adding captions. In this chapter we shall be looking at some of the visual effects available in an online.

2D Effects

Cut

The simplest transition from one shot to another is the straight cut. Around 95% of the time in the vast majority of programs it is the most effective way of editing. Any other transition should only be used if there is a reason for using it. One exception is pop promos where you are likely to want to throw every effect in the book at the production.

Mix

Also referred to as a dissolve, a mix can be used to soften a transition. One picture fades in over another and replaces it. You can often create mixes in an offline and the EDL will read them. You won't need to go through the online assembly re-inserting them. Mixes can be as long or as short as you want them to be. They are timed in terms of frames. So a 12-frame mix will occur in the space of half a second.

Freeze

A freeze is a single frame copied a number of times to create the effect of action freezing on the screen. If you copy the frame 25 times you will end up with a one second freeze. You might want to freeze the final frame of a program and run credits over it. It is often useful to be able to freeze a frame just before starting another effect.

Wipe

One image appears to move up, down or across the screen replacing another. In fact what is happening is an invisible line is travelling across the screen revealing the incoming image and obscuring the outgoing image. This line can be made soft-edge. Wipes can be vertical, horizontal or diagonal. They can also consist of geometric shapes such as a square or a circle. With standard 2D wipes it is important to remember that the whole image is present at full screen size throughout the effect. So if you use a circle wipe, at the start of the effect you will only see a section of the incoming image until it is all revealed. The incoming image has not been squeezed down into a circle shape to be then brought out full frame. For that you will need a 3D effect.

All of the above effects should be standard on any online system. In a tape online a straight cut requires only one play-in machine. For any other 2D effect you will need a minimum of two play-in machines. For anything more complex in a tape online you will need at least one channel of DVE and possibly additional play-in machines.

3D Effects

Most 3D effects are achieved by the editor 'grabbing' an image in the effects channel and then manipulating it. The grabbed image is now on a black key background and a second image can be keyed to it.

We will take a very corny example. You have a shot of someone sitting at a computer screen (Shot A) and you want another image – say a person speaking – (Shot B) to come flying out of the computer screen and end up full screen. This was done to death in the 1980s but it illustrates the principle.

Shot A

The editor grabs Shot B. The editor then squeezes the grabbed image down so that it is roughly the same size as the computer screen on Shot A. Its perspective can be altered so that it matches the angle of the screen in Shot A. The editor can also crop the grabbed image if need be or squeeze it in or out either vertically from the edges or horizontally from the top and bottom. The image is now positioned directly over the computer

Shot B

A and B keyed together

screen on Shot A. It may have become a little distorted but this is inevitable. Once the editor is happy with the start position, the grabbed image can be given a number of intermediate positions for its two second journey to full frame. The editor will also have to decide at what moment it returns to normal perspective and any cropping or squeezing is removed. If it looks as though it might work, the editor says a little prayer and runs the effect.

That's the general idea. This example also illustrates a number of options that are open to you with DVE – squeezing a whole image down, cropping, putting into perspective and flying it out.

The prayer works

You could also grab an image in DVE and slide it in or out of frame. This can work well with a string of graphics and looks classier than a simple wipe. Alternatively, you could make an image fall forward to reveal the one behind. You can spin the picture, tumble it, create the effect of a page turn. You could divide the screen into four quarters and squeeze four images down to create a four-way split with them all running at once. But on a linear online you will need as many play-in machines and effects channels as there are

Picture flies out . . .

. . . and comes full frame

effects running simultaneously on the screen. The only way round that is to build the effect up with a number of **passes**. But the quality will be going down with each pass.

Planning Effects

If you want to achieve a particular effect you have not done before, try and discuss it with the online suite you plan to use before you get in there. It may be their system cannot achieve what you want. If what you are trying to do is particularly demanding it may best to complete that part of the program on a high-end effects system such as Flint, Flame or Henry and then edit the results into your program.

Image Effects

As well as creating transitional effects in the online edit you can also play around with whole shots or sequences in various ways. You can slow down the picture with slo-mo or you can speed it up. On **slo-mo** you can also add a strobe effect which makes a shot look as though it is running as a series of still frames.

As we have already seen you can **flop** a picture from left to right or **flip** it so that is upside down. You can add a coloured **tint** to all or part of a picture. For example you could add blue to a sky by adding a tint to the top third of picture and putting in a soft-edge wipe so that it blends naturally with the rest of the picture. You can **solarise** to give the effect of a negative, **posterise** to give pictures a grainy, shiny look or give an image a **mosaic** effect. You can adjust contrast, light or **luma** levels, colour or **chroma** levels – either to improve a picture or to **knock it back** and create a faded effect. You can also, within limits, **resize** a shot so that you are only seeing part of the picture and the outer edges are not visible. To do this you are blowing the picture up and the quality will suffer slightly. You can also add coloured shapes or borders to pictures.

Estimating Online Time

Online edits almost always take longer than you think they will. And if you book longer than you think you will need, work has a habit of expanding to fill time. Most edit suites are fairly reasonable about this and will agree, for example, to a 4 hour booking with an hour's over-run. If you only use the 4 hours, that's all you will pay for and you know you can go to 5 hours without having the next booking banging on the door demanding to be let in.

Finished program length is one guide to the length of time you will need for both autoconform and online editing but the real determinants are the number of edits, the number of source tapes and the number of effects. A 10-minute program with 100 edits coming off 10 tapes is going to take longer to conform than one the same length with half the number of edits coming off only 2 tapes. Most online suites are able to give you a pretty accurate estimate of time needed based on that kind of information.

Estimating how long it will take to set up and record any visual effects is a little trickier. Most 2D effects are fairly quick to do – so long as you know what you want. 3D effects take longer. The one we looked at above could take anything up to half an hour to get right. A lot will depend on how skilled the editor is. If you are going to be using the same effect a number of times in a program, it can be stored and re-used.

And Finally . . .

An online edit is only over once you have seen it through. Both editor and director should watch the whole program through to make sure there are no technical glitches and all transitions and effects are satisfactory. You will probably have reviewed every edit as you did them but there is almost always something you won't have noticed first time round. This may mean missing your last bus home but it is lot less annoying than having to come back to correct something.

Chapter 17
Post-production Sound

The final soundtrack on any recorded program will be made up of a number of elements. These could include the sync soundtrack recorded at the same time as the pictures, commentary, music, sound effects and buzz tracks. All these elements – or tracks – need to be mixed so that the final soundtrack plays at a constant level and, if two or more tracks are playing at the same time, so that they are all audible. For example, music or background sound might need to be held down so that you can hear a voice-over. Once the voice-over finishes, the level at which the music plays could be brought up. The music might then be dipped again slightly as the voice-over resumes.

The process of editing, selecting and mixing sound tracks is known as a **dub**. For reasons now lost in the mists of time a dub, in the film world, meant a copy of something. And it is still used to refer to a copy of a tape. Presumably because mixing sound used to involve making various copies of soundtracks it is also applied to this process. It's usually obvious in what sense the word is being used. During an online edit the editor might ask – 'will you be dubbing this?' – meaning will you be taking this into a sound suite or dubbing theatre and mixing the sound. Or an editor might ask – 'will you need any dubs of this?' – meaning will you need any copies of this.

There is a very good reason why the online editor will ask the first question. If the sound is relatively straightforward you may want to mix it in the online. Ideally, the editor needs to know this at the start of the edit. If it is a bit more complex you will probably need to take the edit master into a dubbing theatre; in which case the online editor won't do anything to the sound. A program that consisted of a music introduction over opening titles, followed by voice-over and interviews could probably be handled in the online suite.

These are some of the reasons you would need to use a dubbing theatre:

☐ To record voice-over commentary either wild or to picture

☐ To smooth out sound cuts that jar on the ear

☐ To try and improve any location sound that was poorly recorded

☐ To lay down or edit music

☐ To add spot effects

☐ To mix sound where there are more than two tracks playing simultaneously

☐ To produce dubbed foreign language versions

The Process

Dubbing a program is usually the final stage in the post-production process. The dubbing theatre makes a time coded copy of the edit master pictures either onto tape or optical disk. All of the sound tracks that the editor has supplied are then digitised. If the program has been mastered on Beta SP there will be just two tracks and if the editor knows that a dub is planned individual sound clips will have been left long. This gives the dubbing mixer handles to work with. Digibeta allows the option of four separate sound tracks.

If a voice-over is to be recorded this is normally done first. The dubbing mixer then goes through the program to balance all the sound, sorting out any problems, adding any music or effects that are required and making sure that all the tracks sound right together. Once the dubbing mixer and director are satisfied, all the tracks are mixed down to create the final soundtrack.

However, if there is any chance of further work needing to be done on the program – another edit or production of foreign language versions – the dubbing mixer also makes up a separate **M&E** – a music and effects track.

The two sound tracks – the final mix and the separate M&E – are then laid back to the original online edit master. It is important that both the edit master and its box are now labelled correctly showing Final Mix on one track and M&E on another track.

Recording Voice-over

The first step is to choose a voice-over artist. There are a number of types of voice to choose from – the instantly recognisable celebrity, the anonymous professional voice-over artist, a broadcast journalist, your good self or someone you just happened to meet at a party. Forget the last two – they seldom work.

Celebrities will be expensive but they could add a touch of class; though be prepared for the audience muttering to themselves 'I know that voice but I can't think who it is for the moment' as their attention wanders from your beautifully crafted script and pictures. The same could apply with a well-known broadcaster or presenter – if this isn't their normal spot. Most voice-over artists have trained as actors but this doesn't mean all actors can deliver a voice-over or understand the process. Unless you are feeling in a generous mood and want to subsidise someone's on-the-job training, choose a voice-over artist who knows what they are doing.

There are a number of agencies that specialise in offering voice-over artists. Tell them what kind of voice you are looking for and they will usually send you a selection to listen to. Once you have made your choice the agent may ask for a copy of the script to be sent to the artist beforehand. If this isn't convenient, don't get pressured. Most good voice artists don't really expect it and are quite used to picking up a script and reading it as they walk into the suite. Three copies of the script are needed – for the director, the dubbing mixer and the artist. What is important is to brief the artist just before the recording on what kind of performance you are looking for – do you want it hard and punchy, soft and gentle, neutral, committed or whatever.

POST-PRODUCTION SOUND

Most dubbing theatres are set up with a mixer desk and production desk in one room and the actual recording studio or booth where the artist sits next to it. Separating the two rooms will be a soundproofed door and a heavy plate glass window. In both rooms there will be either monitors or large screens. The artist wears cans and will have a cue light on the desk. Communication is by switch talkback from either the dubbing mixer or the director into the artist's cans. The artist talks back to them over the mike. Both the dubbing mixer and the director have a second button to trigger the cue light and let the artist know it's the moment to start recording a line or section of commentary.

A dubbing theatre

It is very rare that an entire commentary is recorded in one take. If you need to stop for some reason – the performance isn't quite right, there's a rustle of papers, etc – you can always go back on the recording and pick it up from the point at which it went wrong. This is known as rock and roll. The artist hears the outgoing recorded commentary on cans and picks up on the next section. If you are recording a voice-over wild and are then going to lay it back to picture in the online edit, you want to be sure it is going to fit. The director will probably have recorded a scratch commentary or guide track in the offline edit. This can be played into the artist's cans as he or she is delivering the final, polished version so the pace and timing match. But warn both the dubbing mixer and the artist before you start that you want to do this.

The better alternative is to record the voice-over to picture. A time coded copy of the edit master is made and played in the dubbing theatre as the artist delivers the commentary. The script can be marked up with the relevant time codes and cue points, the director hits the cue light, the artist keeps one eye on what is happening on the screen and words and pictures match perfectly. The artist is also hearing what else is on your soundtrack and can match voice to the mood you are trying to create. It doesn't matter if you get it wrong. That's what rock and roll is for. The only problem with recording to picture is that it costs more than recording wild and it can take longer. But you will get a better result.

Like an online edit a voice-over recording isn't over until it has been played back in its entirety and everybody is happy with it. If there is still something that needs to be done again, the artist need only record that particular line and it can be dropped in.

Repairing, Improving and Editing

With the voice-over recorded the dubbing mixer can now go through the whole program and see what needs doing to the sound tracks. The offline editor should have noted down any passages of sound that require attention. If there is too much hiss or rumble because someone has been recorded slightly off-mike, that section of the track can be **EQ'd** – or equalised. The imperfections don't disappear completely but can be made far less noticeable. Any sound edits that jar can be smoothed over by improving the cross fade between them or by extending a buzz track to cover them.

Adding Music

The technical side of adding music is fairly straightforward. You choose the music you want and put it where you think it ought to go. The big question is always – what music? There are three sources of program music:

- get it composed so that it works specifically with your program

- use library music

- use a commercial recording.

The cheapest option is the second one – **library music**. There are a number of companies who put together CDs packed with music specially written for video producers and others. Very often they will do a search for you in their collection if there is a particular style of music you after. They also produce catalogues listing everything they have got. If you use a particular track you fill out a form and send it to an organisation called the MCPS (Mechanical-Copyright Protection Society). You are then billed depending on the duration of the tracks used, the number of copies you will be making and where and how it will be shown. It's an honour system and it appears to work. If you can find a track you like, the system is good value for money. But allow lots of time for selecting. Most edit suites have a massive collection of this type of music. If you are lucky you will find something that works. Often the best bet is to use classical music. You can get hold of good recordings with full orchestras of most of the best known classics issued by the music library companies.

Specially composed music is going to cost more but it is often worth the expense. You know what you are getting and there are plenty of composers around who understand about working to picture. It is always best to let the composer see the pictures they are writing for.

If you want to use a **commercial recording** you will have to negotiate with the recording company and the music publisher. Generally, they are helpful. The block that can occur is when they start talking to the group or its agent. They always seem to be in Switzerland and can't be contacted. By and large though something can usually be worked out – but you will probably end up paying as much if not more than you will for getting music composed. But that's why rock stars and their agents are driving around in Rolls Royce and the rest of have to make do with something more modest.

Sound Effects

There are two kinds of sound effect. One is where you distort the existing sound – say adding echo to a voice. The other is where you add a **spot effect**. A spot effect is a sound effect that you either get off disk or create in the studio to add to the background sound of your program – it could be birdsong, traffic noise, a door opening, the clip-clop of horse's hooves, etc. A good effects track can add considerably to the impact of your pictures and is an essential ingredient to creating atmosphere.

Foreign Language Dubs

The process is fairly simple but there are a few things to watch along the way. First you will need to find someone to translate the program. There are a lot of translation agencies around but they don't all understand what is required for a television program. Choose one that knows what is involved and make sure their translators are translating into their mother tongue.

Some translators will only work to a transcript of the program. Others will also be prepared to work to a VHS copy with burnt-in time code plus a transcript. Whichever way they are working they will need a full transcript of everything that is to be translated. This should be laid out in two columns like a script. In the left-hand column make a note of the time codes at the start and end of each sequence – add a brief description of the visuals as well. Use the time code to work out the duration of each sequence and then knock off a few seconds for pauses. Tell the translation agency that each section of the transcript must be translated so that each is no longer than the durations you have shown. Many languages are wordier than English so the translator is going to have to edit the words to get them to fit to your pictures. This is why it is important to choose an agency and translators who understand that their words are going to be read to picture.

It can also be useful to let the translators have any reference material that will show them the style of language you after and translations of any key words – particularly if the English contains jargon or technical language.

Once you have got the hard copy back from the translator you can get a good idea of whether it is going to fit by doing a word count on each section and seeing how it compares with the English. It is a tedious task but it will save a lot of agony in the dub. You may also want to get a second opinion on the translation. If this is a corporate video get the client to run the translation past some of their own people to make sure the style is right.

Now you are going to need a voice or voices to dub the foreign language. As a general rule these should also be native speakers. If you have an interview in French in what is otherwise an English program there is a strong case for getting a bilingual French person to dub it into English. For a start they will have a slight French accent. They will also have a better sense of what is being said in the original interview and they can give a valuable second opinion on the translation itself. If you were dubbing a whole program from English into French, you would probably want to use only French
 artists. Voice-over artists' opinions on the translation are helpful but if your client has signed off on a translation, it can be more trouble than it is worth to start changing it again at the last moment.

If a program consists of a voice-over and a number of interviews, you are going to need at least two voice-over artists – one to do the voice-over and another to do the interviews – assuming all the interviewees are of the same gender. If you have to use a number of voices you will need to decide whether you book them all at the same time for the session or whether you do it in sections. From a cost point of view it is better to bring them in separately. Otherwise you may be paying them to sit around doing nothing.

Finding good foreign language voice-over artists is relatively easy. Most of the translation agencies that specialise in television work also have a string of foreign language voice-over artists on their books. But they tend to be based in major cosmopolitan cities where there is plenty of other work for their talents.

Subtitling

The alternative to dubbing into a foreign language is to add subtitles and it can work out a lot cheaper. It's got nothing to do with post-production sound but as we're on the subject of foreign language versions we'll deal with it here. If you are very sure of what you are doing, you can add subtitles in an online edit using a caption generator. But it is far better to engage the services of a company that specialises in foreign language subtitling. You give them a copy of your edit master plus a full transcript and they get it translated to fit the pictures. They will usually supply you with hard copy and a VHS approval copy. Once you and your client are happy they proceed to make a sub-master with the subtitles added.

One point to consider is that they will be placing the subtitles in the lower third of frame – just where you placed your name supers on the English edit master. So if you are using name supers you will need to re-edit your master and reposition them somewhere else. If you know you are going to want to make subtitled foreign language versions it can often pay to go through this process at the same time as you originally online edit your program.

CHAPTER 18
SAMPLE PRODUCTIONS

So far we have looked mainly at the organisational and technical side of program making. In this chapter we will be looking at the editorial and creative side of the process. One of the principal features of television is that it cuts across a broader range of disciplines than any other medium – journalism, music, drama, sport, comedy and so on. It offers opportunities to exercise a variety of skills and pursue many different interests. So we will be looking at what can happen in the case of a number of different types of production – a news story, a current affairs spot, a corporate video and a drama production.

News

What is news?

It's an event that is happening or that has just happened; an event that is sufficiently important or shocking to excite or interest the maximum number of your potential viewers.

Who decides whether an event meets those criteria? In the first instance it's the editorial team that are running a news program. And the reason they are in that job is that they have what is called 'news sense'. They know what makes a story. They know what their viewers count as news. It's an instinct rather than an acquired skill. If you haven't got it, don't worry. Skip this section and move on. News is only one branch of television. But if you think you know the answer to whether **200 killed in New York plane crash** rates as a bigger story than **2 million die in Chinese famine**, read on . . .

And the answer is – it's the New York plane crash. Why? This is a British news broadcast. There could have been some Brits on board. Even if there weren't, America is closer to Britain than China in terms of distance and culture. Planes aren't meant to crash, particularly not on big cities in America. There are going to be questions. What's more there are going to be pictures.

Sorry if this all sounds a bit cynical but it's the way the news mind needs to work because in fact it's also the way the viewer's mind works. This isn't to say you don't cover the Chinese famine – it is one hell of a story. But the fact is the air crash happened today, you know you can cover it fully, your viewers will want to know what has happened and they will all be asking why did it happen and could it happen to me? So it's the obvious 'lead' to the bulletin.

In practice you may not be faced with choosing between one story and another. On most days there is seldom a big death and disaster story that pushes everything else off the schedule. The truth is that the majority of the news agenda is set several days beforehand. Newsrooms will have advance notice of major government announcements, court cases, economic news and so on. The skill is to decide in advance what is going to be worth covering, what the story is likely to be and what resources to devote to covering it.

Example

In three days time the Health Minister is going to announce 2000 new hospital beds for the National Health Service. How do you cover it?

You know this because the Department of Health has sent out a press release. The minister will make the announcement in Parliament and then give a press conference. Earlier in the day he will be available for a photo opportunity and will walk up and down a gleaming new ward surrounded by men and women in white coats.

If you know all of this why don't you tell people about it right now? The reason you don't is because there is an embargo on the press release. You are not at liberty to broadcast its contents until a specific time on a specific day. If this sounds like news management, it is. But it is not that sinister. The arrangement suits everybody. Without an embargo system which everybody respects, planning news coverage would become impossible.

What the minister would like is a 'good news' story of him making the announcement and then to be seen surrounded by grateful patients and doctors. But journalists are rightly suspicious of good news stories. For a very good reason. Good news is very seldom the whole story. You start to ask yourself a few questions – are these really 'new' beds and where is the money coming from? You make a few phone calls – to the opposition party – what's their reaction going to be – to the health unions – will there be the staff to operate the new beds? They may be on to you already putting their side of the story – with their own embargoed press releases.

What they are saying suggests this whole business isn't as simple as the minister would like you to think it is. You have now got a story. You set up interviews with the opposition, the health union and the minister and arrange coverage of the minister's hospital ward walkabout. You're all set for a three minute package that's going to be the lead story that day.

Everything goes according to plan. Your soundbites are good. Your pictures are fine. You shoot an opening piece to camera with the minister's walkabout going on in the background and a closing piece outside the Treasury saying something like 'but the people here still can't tell us where the money is coming from'. And you get it all ready in time for the first evening bulletin.

Then, with an hour to go before transmission, news comes in of the New York air crash. As your colleagues start putting together a package of the pictures coming in from the United States, you're told your piece has been cut to one minute and will be run somewhere near the end of the bulletin. Get down to editing and chop it down. Drop the top and tail pieces to camera, rewrite and revoice the intro over the walkabout shots, keep the minister and the opposition spokesman but drop the health union spokesman. Done. Sorted. That's news.

Current Affairs Item

The way you approach producing a current affairs item will be similar to the way a news item is dealt with. The difference is that you will probably be giving a topic more airtime and examining it in a bit more depth. But don't get carried away. There's only so much that can be said in ten minutes and you are unlikely to be able to explain all the intricacies of European Monetary Union in that time. The trick is to get at the essentials and to present a complex subject in such a way that it is understandable to the average viewer.

Quite who the average viewer is no one really knows. Some producers say to themselves – 'Would my Mum know what this is all about or be interested in it?.' This is fine, if a little patronising, so long as Mum doesn't happen to an Emeritus Professor of Economics. If she is, you might need to think instead of her sister who stayed at home and brought up three kids in Bromley with her insurance salesman husband. Would you be pitching the item right for them as they sip their cocoa idly watching your program before putting the cat out for the night? It's not a bad yardstick.

There are well-established formats for current affairs items. Broadly speaking you can either cover a topic with a self-contained package consisting largely of material shot on location or with a briefer package that introduces the item followed by a studio interview or discussion. In terms of content you will be trying to do a number of things:

•   explain the background to what may be a complex issue

•   reveal facts that may not already be known

•   present the arguments on both sides of an issue.

To do that successfully you need to be able to look at an issue from all points of view yourself. You may have strong views of your own. Try and keep them to yourself. This isn't just because your broadcast organisation is obliged to produce 'balanced' programming. It is also because a one-sided item will end up being a big turn off for the viewers. People who watch current affairs programs tend to have strong views themselves. What they want to see is their side giving the other side a verbal duffing up. The moment they start to feel they are being subjected to propaganda they will switch off and watch something else.

You also need to maintain a clear focus on the topic you are dealing with. Take the example of European Monetary Union. It's a huge and complex subject. You cannot expect to do it justice in one item or even a whole program. So you need to try to boil it down to a single question – 'Will EMU mean we are all richer/poorer?' or 'Will EMU mean we will all pay taxes to Brussels?' – and then address that question. These are the sort of questions your viewers want answered – they're also the sort of questions that politicians will hate answering. If that's the case, you're clearly on the right track. You are performing a useful public service and producing good television.

Once you have settled on the question, you need to find the people to give you the opposing answers. These could be politicians, academics or leaders of pressure groups. Whatever route you choose to go they need to be people who can lay claim to some expertise on the subject and who are prepared to take a clear line. You don't want people who sit there saying 'on the one hand, on the other hand'. You will probably have done something like that yourself in the package that introduces the discussion. Any issue that people are interested in is also one that people feel strongly about. Your item needs to reflect some of that emotion and passion. The viewers expect it and won't thank you for an arid exposition of purely rational arguments.

Corporate Video

Corporate videos – made on behalf of companies or organisations – come in all shapes and sizes and are made for a variety of purposes. By and large they fall into two categories:

- videos made for external use, principally commissioned by sales, marketing and public relations departments

- videos made for internal use to meet an organisation's in-house communication or training needs.

The major difference between any corporate video and a broadcast program is that the producer has no editorial independence and is doing entirely what the client demands. However, a corporate video that comes across as straight propaganda and that oversells its message won't work. The viewers will quickly see through it. Part of a corporate video producer's skill is in presenting messages both positively and convincingly. Is the program going to consist of the company chairman talking straight to camera telling everyone what a wonderful company they work for or might it not be better to have him interviewed by someone who is putting questions on behalf of the workforce? The second way of doing it will produce a program that is both more watchable and more credible. A corporate video producer needs to gain the trust of the client and persuade them of the format that will in the end work best for them.

Coming up with successful formats for corporate videos can be creatively demanding. Clients will often want an original approach. At the same time they can be frightened off by something that is too wacky. Often the trick is to take a recognised broadcast format and then adapt it. A news magazine for a company might well have the look of a broadcast breakfast show or evening current affairs program, even down to using the same presenters. Or you might want to use a game show format. But be careful. Check first you are not infringing anyone's copyright. If you can think of a way of communicating messages through visual imagery, so much the better. Every international company wants to see a spinning globe at some point in its program. It's not original but it says visually what they and you want to communicate.

Corporate videos are invariably script-led. On the client side everyone wants to see as full a script as possible at as early a stage as possible. Clients will tend only to read the right-hand side of the script – the words – and not take in what is going to be happening visually. It is often a good idea to talk a client through a script explaining what the video will both look and sound like. You may need to talk them out of packing the commentary full of facts for which no pictures exist. Clients may often think they want interviews to be scripted in advance. Try and dissuade them from this approach. Pre-scripted soundbites seldom sound natural or convincing. Suggest instead that you write a summary of what is to be said for the interviewee to then deliver in their own words.

Corporate producers stay in business for two reasons:

- they produce programs their clients like on time and on budget

- they get on with their clients and successfully manage their relationships with them.

If the producer is not also the director and writer and is employing freelances, a judgement has to be made about the extent to which they are involved with the client. Scriptwriters and directors may not have the best interpersonal skills when it comes to dealing with clients. It can often be best for the producer to act as the go-between at the pre-production stage and later when it comes to showing the finished work to the client. During shooting it can often be important to impress on camera crews that the client is paying for this production and they should avoid doing or saying anything that will upset the client. Try not to disrupt offices and workplaces for the sake of that extra special shot. It won't be appreciated. You have a job to do but so do the people you are shooting.

Very few corporate clients know very much about the technical process of program making. They need to be steered through it and made aware of what is possible and what is not possible – within the budget. It is also important for the producer to establish a single point of contact within the client organisation. If a producer is having to deal with a number of different people within the company, wires can get fatally crossed. This is particularly important when it comes to setting up shooting and interviews at different locations. If Head Office haven't told a remote sales office that you are coming to shoot on a given day, you won't get in and it will end up being your fault not the client's.

Drama

For most program makers producing drama is one of the most demanding and at the same time most satisfying forms of television. The key to producing good drama lies in a good script, good teamwork, detailed planning – and good actors.

We will assume you already have a good script to work with. Teamwork happens when everyone knows what they are expected to do and when they are expected to do it. If they are professionals and they have been told both those things, they will do it. Detailed planning means setting a realistic schedule and making sure you have the sets or locations, the make-up, the costumes, the props, the vehicles and anything else you need where you want it, when you are likely to need it. In other words, the recipe is the same as for any successful production. The only difference is that you are managing a lot more ingredients. So we will concentrate in this section on how you find good actors and how you can work with them to produce the best results.

The best way to find good actors is to hire the services of a casting director. Your brief to the casting director should include a description of the production, the ages, gender and character of the parts you want to cast and the rate you are prepared to pay. The casting director will usually find you five or six different actors they judge might be suitable for each part and get them in for an audition.

You might decide you want to see the actors' photographs and CVs first and make a pre-selection. This is not advised. Actors seldom really look like their photographs. Their CVs never tell you their ages and their list of credits may not mean a lot to you unless you actually saw the production they appeared in. And until you meet them you won't know what they sound like or whether they match up with the character you have in mind.

Very often the first you will see of an individual actor's CV will be at the audition. The first thing to look for on the CV is to see whether they have done any television. Television acting is different from theatre acting and requires an understanding of the medium. Actors aren't taught much about television at most drama schools.

So if it comes to a narrow choice between two actors – go for the one with the experience of television techniques.

By the time you get to auditioning actors, the script should be well advanced if not complete. Get each actor to read a scene or two of their part, reading other parts yourself if necessary. If they can do it well with you as a foil, they are probably going to be pretty good. In most instances you won't have sent them the script in advance. Good actors can pick up a script and get the hang of what is required pretty quickly – in much the same way as a musician can scan a sheet of music and play it. But before you get them to read, explain something of the kind of production and the character they are reading for. If they take it on board, you will know whether they are on your wavelength and will take direction on the shoot. If they don't, it may be your fault, but either way this relationship is not going to work. You may also want them to walk, move about or perform some action that will be required in the production. At some point get them to talk about other work they have done that might be similar to your production.

Make sure you have a visual record of each actor you see – either a Polaroid or, if the budget will stretch to it, shoot them on video. If you allow around 15 minutes for each actor, you could be seeing over 20 different actors for different parts in the course of one day and you can easily forget who was who by the end of it. Make notes on each one immediately after you have seen them.

There are alternatives to this casting method. There is nothing to stop you going direct to a number of actors' agents and ask them who they have got that meets your requirements. The only problem is that they may tell you all their people are wonderful and your choice will be limited to the people they have on their books.

If there is a particular actor you know you want or that you have worked with before then you can go direct to their agent. In the UK all actors who are members of Equity are listed in Spotlight. You can call Spotlight and they will give you the number of the actor's agent. But you should always see the actor you have in mind before booking them. People change. That brilliant actor you saw on TV or worked with two years ago could have had three nervous breakdowns since, is drinking a bottle of whisky a day and has put on 30 pounds.

Once you have completed casting, always try and rehearse with the actors before you shoot. You will have to pay them for rehearsal time but it can work out a lot cheaper than rehearsing on the shoot; when you are also paying for your full crew, studio and whatever else. Rehearsal also means that by the time you are shooting, performance issues will have been largely resolved.

Different directors have different ways of rehearsing. The classic way is to read through the script so that everyone is familiar with it and gets an idea of how they are meant to interact with the other characters. Some discussion between the director and the actors as to the characters can be useful. Each actor needs to know how the director sees the character they are playing, what sort of person and what sort of attitudes or emotions they are meant to be portraying. The actors also need to know their moves. The director should have blocked these out – as well as the camera positions – before rehearsal. Equally the actors should have come to rehearsal with their lines learnt. They should have them off pat by the time it comes to shooting.

That's just a brief overview of what's involved in producing drama and working with actors. The only other thing to remember is that when actors do something the way you want it and get it right, they do like to be told how well they've done.

Chapter 19
Working as a Freelance

This chapter is intended for anyone thinking of working as a freelance in the UK. It addresses some of the key issues you will need to be considering and suggests various approaches.

Working as a freelance is not for everyone. It is insecure. You can never predict what you will be working on. You may not know from one day to the next whether you have got any work at all. You can never be sure how much or how little you are going to be earning. Unlike a salaried employee in an established company, you won't get a company car, paid holidays, medical insurance or a guaranteed pension. You will have to market yourself and you will have to do all your own administration. You will be responsible for paying all your taxes. So why would anyone want to put themselves through all that misery?

People decide to work on a freelance basis for a number of reasons. It may be there are few permanent jobs on offer for their particular set of skills. It could be that they prefer temperamentally not to work full-time for one employer. They may have been made redundant from a full-time job and reckon that working freelance is the best way back into the job market. They may take the view that they will have a more varied and interesting work pattern or that they will have more free time and opportunities to earn more.

If you decide you want to work as a freelance you need to ask yourself:

☐ who is likely to employ you – what is your market?

☐ how do you let your market know you are around?

☐ how much should you charge?

☐ are you set up to handle the money side of things?

Who is Going to Employ You?

The answer will vary slightly depending on what particular skills you are offering.

- A writer or director should be targeting production companies or broadcast producers.

- An editor would need to target edit facilities but should also build up and maintain contacts with directors who will often be in a position to ask for and get a particular editor.

- A camera operator or sound recordist might target crewing facilities or agencies and, again, maintain contact with directors.

So the guiding principle is to think about who actually signs on people with your particular skills and then also think about people who are likely to recommend you or ask for you.

Letting People Know you are Around

There are a number of different ways freelances let potential employers know they around. Mail-outs, cold calls, directory listings and reminders to past clients are just a few. The brutal truth is that it mostly happens by word of mouth. This is less easy to make happen but it doesn't require any effort.

Whatever route you choose, you are going to need an up to date and relevant **CV**. Try to limit it to two sides of paper at most and keep its appearance as simple and readable as possible. Make sure it features productions you have been involved with, what you have done and who you have worked for. You may also need to put together a **showreel** featuring your best work. Even if you don't mail out your **CV** or showreel you may be asked for them.

If you do decide a **mail-out** is going to be worthwhile, who should you send your **CV** to? There are numerous **industry directories** that will list the companies who might want to employ you. Spend some time going through the directories sorting out what type of company is your best bet. You may find that one directory or another contains a section featuring freelances with your skill set. If so, try and get yourself listed in their next edition. It probably won't cost you anything.

Mailing your **CV** out to a host of different companies addressed to The Producer or The Production Manager might produce results but you will increase your chances of success if your **CV** is going direct to the person most likely to give you work. Sometimes the directory you may have used to get your addresses will also list individuals. But they may not be the people you need to be talking to or the details could be out of date. Why not phone up the company, tell them you're a freelance whatever and you'd like to know who you should send your details to. This is often a good way of making a **cold call** that doesn't sound like a cold call. You never know. You could be straight through to the very person you need to talk to and you are just what they are looking for at that moment. It doesn't often happen but when it does, you save a lot on stamps and address labels.

If you have done a mail-out without phoning anyone first, it can be worth following up with a phone call a few days afterwards. Don't leave it too long. Don't expect any written replies to mail-outs. The most you can hope for is that somebody files it and looks at it again sometime.

Don't forget your **existing clients** in the rush to sign on new ones. If you have worked for someone in the past and haven't heard from them for a while, give them a call and/or drop them a line bringing them up to date on what you have been doing since.

Credits on a broadcast program can often help to get your name known. Try and make sure your name is on any publicity material that a producer is putting out to the trade press.

Deciding your Rate

Once you have got in to see a potential client or taken a phone call asking if you are available one of the first questions you will be asked is what you charge. Once upon a time there used to be an easy answer to this. All you had to say was 'the union rate'. Life is not quite so simple nowadays. In theory, you can charge what you want to charge and clients can pay what they feel like paying. In practice, though, there is usually a market rate for a particular set of skills depending on the type of production. To decide what rate you think you might be able to charge, ask around and see what other people with the same skills are charging.

Rates are usually calculated on a daily basis. If you think you might get more work than everyone else by charging a lot less per day than everyone else, think again. If you are too cheap, clients will wonder whether you are any good. Even if they do give you lots of work, you are then going to find it very difficult to raise your rate later to the market rate.

Bear in mind that when clients ask you what you charge, they will always have a figure in their mind of what they're expecting to pay. If your rate is roughly in line with that, they'll either accept it or tell you what they will pay. It is then up to you to decide whether to accept the rate they are offering or hold out for more and risk losing the work. One solution can be to say you base fees on a daily rate of so much but it depends on the total number of days or weeks. This allows both parties to agree an overall fee that everyone is happy with.

As a general rule it is accepted that editors, camera operators and all technical crew are paid **overtime** on hours worked beyond the agreed normal day. Freelance producers, writers and directors tend not to get paid overtime but it is always worth asking for more than the normal daily rate if weekend work is involved.

On some feature film productions, and very occasionally elsewhere, a producer might want freelances to **work for points**. What this means is that instead of receiving a flat fee, freelances get a percentage of the profits that the production actually makes. This is fine if the production is a roaring success. But you don't know whether it will be. It is also fine so long as the production company that owns the production stays in business. Again, you have no guarantee that it will. So be warned. But don't complain if you refused points and opted for a flat fee and the production then goes on to make millions.

Administration

Some minimal administration is essential if you are working as a freelance. You must make it easy for clients to contact you. That may mean having a separate phone line at home, a mobile phone and/or a pager. You will probably need a fax and you may need to be on e-mail.

A computer is not essential but you will need to have a system for recording the days you are booked for and by whom, the days you have worked and for whom, what you have earned, what you are owed and what you have spent in the course of working. You will need to record all this information both for yourself and for the taxman.

Purchase orders: once you have been commissioned to do some work it may be advisable to get a written confirmation of the order, particularly if you are working for someone for the first time. For a start this puts on paper the rate that has been agreed and avoids any ugly disputes later. More importantly, if you have any difficulty getting the client to pay up and have to go to court, you may need to produce some evidence that the client did in fact commission the work. If your client is too lazy, too busy or too dishonest to give you a purchase order, you will need to make a judgement as to whether you are prepared to risk working without one. If you can't get a purchase order, one small safeguard is to put on paper to the client your understanding of the arrangement. In practice a lot of work happens without anyone writing anyone else purchase orders. This not a particularly satisfactory state of affairs but it is part of the culture of the industry. A lot is done on trust.

Invoices: if you are truly a freelance – rather than someone engaged on a short-term contract – you won't get paid until you have sent your client an invoice. Even then you can expect to wait at least a month until you see your money. Normally you would expect to invoice at the end of the job so the golden rule is:

Get your invoice in quickly.

If you leave it a couple of weeks you will wait that much longer for your money. If a job looks as though it is going to run over several weeks or months tell the client you will be submitting invoices at various stages. If they baulk at this and tell you to wait until the very end of the project and won't be paying out anything until then, go away and have a big think about whether you really want to commit to working for these people.

An invoice needs to contain the following information:

☐ Your name, address and telephone number

☐ The name and address of the company you are invoicing and the name of the person who commissioned the work

☐ The date

☐ A summary of the work carried out

☐ The fee being charged

☐ If you are registered for VAT, the amount of VAT being charged and your VAT number

☐ The total amount due (i.e. the fee – the net amount – plus the VAT)

☐ Your credit terms – the number of days that may elapse before the invoice is due for settlement

Credit terms: most freelances give their clients 30 days to pay. In theory these 30 days are designed to give the client time to process the invoice, clear it through their own system, raise a cheque, get it authorised and signed, put it in an envelope and send it out to you. If the client is waiting for payment from their client they should also have got their money in by then.

The awful truth is that your 30 days doesn't actually mean a lot. It is not legally enforceable and some clients may turn round to you after the event and say 'we only pay on 60 days or even 90 days'. Before you accept work it is worth asking how quickly you can expect your invoice to be settled. Depending on the answer, you may need to start sending the client written reminders or telephoning their accounts department once the invoice is due. If the client has a reputation for being a slow payer, don't be afraid to badger them. If you are in a position to choose, try and work only for people who pay on time.

Keeping Records

As well as keeping a record of everything you have been paid, and what is due, you will also need to keep a record of what you spend in the course of working. This could include stationery, computer supplies, telephone bills, petrol. You should be able to claim most of these expenses against your income when it comes to calculating what tax you have to pay. You may also be able to claim for the use of a room at home to work from and some of the cost of buying assets such as a car and a computer. You can, if you wish, do all these calculations yourself and deal direct with the Inland Revenue for income tax and Customs and Revenue for VAT. Most people prefer to engage an accountant to do all or part of this for them. Even so, you will need to keep accurate records yourself so that your accountant has the right information to work with.

Administration Checklist

☐ Make it easy for people to contact you

☐ Get confirmation of orders

☐ Get your invoice in quickly

☐ Chase up slow payers

☐ Keep accurate, up-to-date records

Choosing an Accountant

As a general rule it is advisable only to consider using a fully qualified Chartered Accountant. People calling themselves simply certified accountant or accountant are to be avoided. As with anything else, it is best first to ask around and talk to people you know, ask who they use and whether they would recommend using the same person.

If they are happy with the service they are receiving, go and see that particular accountant. Most accountants will offer a first meeting free of charge. If they spend all their time telling you what a great job they do and how they will save you lots of tax, don't get too excited. You are going to be better off with someone who is actually trying to understand what you do, how your business works and what your needs will be. So look for someone who is asking you intelligent questions about your business and who demonstrates they actually understand what you are saying. Try and establish who will actually be doing the work. Will it be the person you are actually talking to or will it all be done by a trainee? If it is going to be someone else, ask to meet them.

If you go and talk to two or three accountants you will probably find the advice they are offering is fairly similar. What really counts is the quality of the service. How long do they take from receipt of all the information you will be sending them to preparing accounts for submission to the Inland Revenue? Can you call up at any time for advice? Do they issue bulletins, summaries of tax changes, etc. If so, ask to see the sort of information they send out on a regular basis. And, of course, what does the service cost? Try and get them to agree to a fixed annual fee. Make sure they tell you in advance if any additional work could mean you are charged more than the annual fee.

As well as taking all these factors into account, your final decision will also depend on whether you feel comfortable with the person you are dealing with – and whether they explain what they will be doing on your behalf in language you understand.

Book-keeping Basics

Your accountant is unlikely to be keeping detailed, accurate, up-to-date records of all your income and expenditure. This is something you are going to have to do for yourself, unless you also want to pay for the services of a book-keeper.

You can either keep manual, handwritten records or put everything on a computer. On a computer you can either use an off-the-shelf accounts package or set up a number of spreadsheets. Whichever you use, you will need to understand some of the basic principles of book-keeping. And it is easiest to understand book-keeping in terms of two separate ledgers – your sales ledger which records all sales and income – and your bought ledger which records all expenditure. If you are starting from scratch get your accountant to show you how this information should be recorded and the details that will be required. As far as expenditure is concerned, your accountant will probably want you to record it so that it is easy to see how much in total you have spent under individual headings such as stationery or travel.

VAT

If your turnover (the total you earn before deducting expenses) is over a certain amount per quarter or per year you will need to register for VAT and add VAT to all the fees you are charging when you invoice clients. It can be a good idea to do this anyway for image reasons. If you are selling yourself as top-flight director who might just be able to fit in another job before flying off to shoot a commercial in the Caribbean, your story isn't going to look too good if your invoice shows you don't charge VAT. If you do charge VAT it is no skin off the client's nose. They will be registered and be able to claim back the VAT you have charged. Similarly, you will be able to claim back the VAT on goods and services you have had to purchase in the course of your work.

The downside of VAT is that you have to file a return once a quarter showing the VAT you have earned and the VAT you have spent. Not only that, but you have to hand over the difference in the form of a cheque for what you owe. Don't try to get clever with the VAT people. They come and inspect you soon after you have registered to make sure you are doing everything properly and they'll be back again periodically to make sure you are still behaving yourself. Play fair with them and they'll play fair with you. They'll even advise you on what you could be claiming for if you are not already doing so.

And Finally . . .

Not everything you earn is yours to keep or spend. Unlike your friends with jobs whose employers pay their tax for them every month, you've got to pay your own tax bills both to the Inland Revenue and maybe the VAT too. So put enough aside for those unhappy moments. And don't forget – one day you may want to retire. You'll need to think about a pension.

CHAPTER 20
GOOD HOUSEKEEPING

If you have got this far in the book you will know that television programs don't get made without a degree of planning, organisation and paperwork. You won't just get by with flair, imagination and creativity – important as they are. There are a few housekeeping habits that are worth developing to save yourself a lot of time, agony and frustration.

Tapes

Throughout a production you need to keep track of your tapes. You need to know where they are and what is on each of them. Every tape should be clearly labelled – at the time of shooting – with the following information:

• Working title

• Roll number

• Date

• Production company

In addition you may want to add details such as names of director and/or camera operator, the location(s) and the client, if applicable. But the four pieces of information above are essential. And make sure the same information is written on both the cassette and its case.

Keep a log of all tapes generated in the course of a production. This is in addition to your shooting log. You won't just be shooting from day to day on location. You are also likely to have graphics and rostrum tapes. The log doesn't need to be complicated – it's just a list of each tape you have shot and a brief summary of what is on each one. The tape log should also tell you where individual tapes are at a given moment – transfer suite, in the office, at the offline edit or wherever. Try and keep all tapes and any other bits and pieces such as music CDs or pieces of artwork together in one box for one production. If items get split up for any reason, show on the log where they have been sent to and when they moved.

If you don't label tapes clearly and you don't have any record of where they have got to, it is not hard to imagine what can go wrong. If you have got one tape and you don't know what is on it you can take a quick look at it – assuming you have a Beta SP machine handy. No machine available and you are in trouble. If you have got twenty unidentified tapes to look at you're going to have waste/spend a day looking though them. If you have no idea where a particular tape is – and it hasn't been properly labelled – you are going to have a hard time finding it.

Once a production is completed the edit master or a sub-master should be stored indefinitely. You never know whether you are going to need it again. As far as rushes are concerned, a lot will depend on what is on them. If there is material you think will be needed again for a re-edit or that can be used in other programs then hang on to everything. You may even have shots you can sell to a stock shot library. You will need to make a judgement about how long you hold material for. In practice, you will probably go though tapes every two years or so and clear out anything you are certain you will never need again. So hang on to your written logs of what is on all your rushes. You may need to refer to it.

Showreel

Always make sure you have examples of your work available. At the very least try and make sure you have a VHS copy of everything you have done. Even better is to have material on Beta SP so you can put together a showreel.

Contacts

Keep a note of everyone you work with – names, numbers, addresses, what they do – and what they are like. You never know when you might need them again. Industry directories only tell you so much. Your own contacts file will become your best source of information.

Music

Make a note of the source and titles of any music tracks you use. You may find you want to re-use the same music in different programs. You'll save yourself endless hours of hunting through CDs if you have a written record to refer to.

Budgets

If you are responsible for making sure a program comes in on budget you will need to have a system for accurately recording what was budgeted for individual budget lines and what was actually spent. If nothing else, it will give you a good guide for getting it right next time.

Trade Press

Even if you don't buy or subscribe to any of the numerous papers and magazines produced for the industry (see Chapter 22), try and flick through them whenever you see them. They will often contain the occasional tip, gossip or idea that can prove useful.

Chapter 21
Shooting and Editing on Film

The grammar and techniques of shooting and editing on film are basically the same as those for shooting on tape. The major difference is that the results can be much better – both in terms of pictures and sound. There are also several important differences in the process. We will look first of all at how a film shoot differs from a tape shoot.

The Shoot

A minimum of three technicians are needed for a film shoot:

- Camera operator

- Camera assistant or clapper/loader

- Sound recordist

You need each of these people because of three important differences between film and tape:

1   Unexposed film stock comes in cans (circular tins about an inch deep). It has to be removed from the can without exposing it to the light and then loaded into the camera's magazine. The magazine is then slotted back onto the camera. Once that roll has been used, the magazine is removed from the camera and the roll is replaced in the can which is sealed with gaffer tape and labelled with a roll number, working title, etc. The loading and unloading of the magazine is performed by the camera assistant using a lightproof black bag made of black cloth. The bag has too short inside-out arms with elasticated wrists into which the camera assistant thrusts their own hands. A camera assistant loading or unloading a magazine is effectively working blind. It is best to start the day with two magazines already loaded. That way there is usually always one ready to use.

2   As well as performing the loading function the camera assistant also operates the clapperboard. The clapperboard or slate is used to show the scene or shot and take number. It should also show the working title and names of the director and camera operator. The clapper bit of it is needed so that sound and picture can be matched up later to run in sync.

The reason for this is that the camera is only shooting pictures while sound is recorded separately. There is an ancient news system for shooting both sound and picture in the camera but you are unlikely to encounter it.

3   This explains why a separate sound recordist is also needed on a film shoot. As well as operating a mixer the sound recordist is also operating a portable tape recorder. There is no cabling between the camera and the tape recorder. The sound recordist can take up an advantageous position without needing to be too close to the camera.

Because of the way film is shot this is what has to happen. At the start of each take the camera assistant shows the camera the clapperboard which in its lower part displays the current shot number and take number. The assistant calls out the number and – if it is a sync shot – claps the upper part of the board down on the lower part. This gives the editor a clear visual and audio point at which to sync up the rushes. If for any reason there isn't time to get a board on the front of a shot it can be end-boarded. The convention then is to offer the board to the camera upside down

If you get to shoot on film you will probably find that clapperboards have moved on a bit since the basic one shown here and now have all kinds of clever digital displays for the numbers and electronic beeps for the sync point. But the principle is the same.

If you are shooting a pop promo you will probably be shooting the artists miming to a playback tape of their original studio recording. The playback tape should be time coded and you can then use a clapperboard that displays that time code. At the moment the board is clapped the editor can match up the playback tape with the picture and with a bit of luck it will look as though the artists are singing in sync – assuming they even turned up for the shoot.

Processing and Transfers

With shooting complete the exposed negative is processed and the sound tapes are transferred to magnetic stock of the same format as your film stock. What happens next depends on whether you want to edit on film, on tape or a mixture of both.

Editing on Tape

Your negative or **neg** is synced up with your transferred sound and both are then transferred via a **telecine** machine to either Beta SP or Digibeta with the picture as a positive image. At the same time a continuous time code is generated. To keep costs down you can have all your material transferred on a **one light** telecine in which case it won't be graded to deal with any light or colour imperfections.

You can now proceed to offline edit as you would normally. Once you are happy with the offline, the clips you know you want to use can be telecined back onto tape with a full or fine grade to give the best quality pictures achievable. The online edit master is then assembled from these tapes.

At each stage the time code generated at the initial telecine transfer acts as the reference for what is to be transferred and how it is to be assembled. It is usually advisable to get the clips you need transferred with handles – a bit over either end – so that there is sufficient material at the start and end of each clip for the online editor to work with.

Editing on Film

Your neg is processed and the lab runs off a **work print** – again this is an ungraded version of your pictures. The editor – or more likely the assistant editor – then syncs up all the pictures with the sound track which has been transferred separately – using the clapperboard as the reference. Each shot is then broken down and marked with its clapperboard number using a white chinagraph.

The editor now assembles the program – physically cutting the work print and the soundtrack and splicing shots together in the order they are going to run. Most film editors prefer to work without the director sitting there telling them what to do. The director will probably have viewed the rushes with the editor, before they are broken down and should have supplied the editor with a paper edit of the program. The paper edit gives the editor an idea of the structure of the program and the shots that the director thinks will work best for each sequence.

The editor's first cut is known as a **rough cut**. There is not a lot of point in cutting a film too accurately at the first attempt. If either editor or director want to change anything it can be very time consuming going back and finding individual frames and splicing them back in again. Once everyone is happy with the rough cut and changes have been agreed, the editor proceeds to produce a **fine cut**.

This cutting copy – compiled from the work print – is now sent off to the **neg cutter** and the neg is cut to match it. Each frame on the neg bears a unique **edge number** and these numbers will have been printed onto the work print frame for frame as it was first run off. The neg cutter reads off the edge numbers on the cutting copy and uses the identical numbers on the neg to assemble the **cut neg**.

From the cut neg the lab now makes an **answer print**. This is usually a graded print. The editor views the answer print both to check that the neg cutters have got it right – seldom a problem – and also to check whether any further grading is necessary. The labs then produce the final **show print**.

Visual effects can be added optically by the lab but the cost is likely to compare unfavourably with the same effects achieved electronically in a tape online. As everything that is produced for television is invariably transmitted from tape this is probably the route to go. In which case, as you will see below, you may not need an answer print or show print.

Meanwhile there is still the small matter of sound to deal with. During the edit the editor has probably only been able to work with one or two sound tracks simultaneously. All the tracks needed for the program need to be laid against the cutting copy and the whole lot will need to be taken into a dubbing theatre to be mixed – just as on tape. The final mixed soundtrack is then laid back against the show print.

Editing on film is a very tactile and time-consuming business. But because the process all takes time – and because editors usually don't have to work with directors pacing up and down the room behind them or drumming their fingers on the desk beside them – the results are often a lot classier than anything that is achieved on tape. Most of the costs are higher to start with and it is not as easy to budget for.

Editing on Film and Tape

There is nothing to stop you doing part of the job on film and part on tape. You might decide to offline on tape, get the neg cut to match the offline but with handles and then telecine the cut neg onto tape at the online. That way you cut out the need for a second transfer to tape and an autoconform. A lot will depend on how much grading needs to be done as you telecine and the relative cost of using an online with telecine.

CHAPTER 22
FURTHER INFORMATION

Trade Magazines

AV MAGAZINE

MacLaren House
19 Scarbrook Road
Croydon, Surrey CR9 1QH
0171-611-0566

Covers business-to-business use of audio visual communications including presentations, video, multimedia, videoconferencing, film, business TV networks and live events.

BROADCAST

33–39 Bowling Green Lane
London EC1R 0DA
0171-505-8014

Weekly newspaper of the TV and radio industry.

CREATION

30–31 Islington Green
London N1 8DU
0171-226-8525

Written for program and film makers with in-depth features on creative and cultural issues.

CUTS

48 Carnaby Street
London W1V 1PF
0171-437-0801

Aimed at producers and post production companies seeking opportunities in Europe and United States.

POST UPDATE

30–31 Islington Green
London N1 8DU
0171-226-8525

Business magazine for the post-production industry with product news and technology updates.

SCREEN INTERNATIONAL

33–39 Bowling Green Lane
London EC1R 0DA
0171-505-8101

Weekly news magazine for global film, television and multimedia business.

TELEVISION

100 Gray's Inn Road
London WC1X 8AL
0171-430-1000

Examines current topics of debate in the industry.

TELEVISUAL

St Giles House, 50 Poland St
London W1V 4AX
0171-439-4222

Monthly covering all aspects of production and post-production in all sectors.

Trade Directories

BFI FILM & TELEVISION HANDBOOK

21 Stephen Street
London W1P 2LN
0171-255-1444

Comprehensive statistical review of the year plus wide range of industry listings and contacts.

BROADCAST PRODUCTION GUIDE

33–39 Bowling Green Lane
London EC1R 0DA
0171-505-8333

Directory of companies involved in all aspects of the UK broadcasting industry.

CONTACTS

7 Leicester Place
London WC2H 7BP
0171-437-5881

Mainly stage, theatre and television related listings. Includes rehearsal rooms and theatrical agents.

KAYS PRODUCTION MANUALS

Pinewood Studios
Pinewood Road, Iver Heath
Bucks SL0 ONH
01608-677222

Range of UK and European production manuals.

KEMPS FILM TV & VIDEO HANDBOOKS

34–35 Newman Street
London W1P 3PD
0171-637-3663

International handbook covering production companies, facilities and services in 54 countries. Also separate UK guide and North American guides.

THE KNOWLEDGE

Riverbank House, Angel Lane
Tonbridge TN9 1SE
01732-362666

Full listings of companies and crews. Also available – The Pocket Knowledge.

PACT DIRECTORY OF INDEPENDENT PRODUCERS

45 Mortimer Street
London W1N 7TP
0171-331-6000

Details of over 400 feature film and independent television production companies.

SPOTLIGHT

7 Leicester Place
London WC2H 7BP
0171-437-5881

Casting directories for actors and presenters.

THE WHITE BOOK

The White Book, Bank House
23 Warwick Road
Coventry CV1 2EW
01203-559 658

International directory to the entertainment, leisure, record, concert, film, video, conference and exhibitions industries.

Trade Organisations

BRITISH FILM INSTITUTE (BFI)

21 Stephen Street
London W1P 2LN
0171-255-1444

Exists to encourage the development of film, television and video in the UK.

BROADCASTING ENTERTAINMENT CINEMATOGRAPH & THEATRE UNION (BECTU)

111 Wardour Street
London W1V 4AY
0171-437-8506

Broadcasting trade union. Operates a Student Link-Up scheme.

DIRECTORS GUILD

15–19 Great Titchfield Street
London W1P 7FB
0171-436-8626

Trade union and crafts guild representing directors working in all media.

INTERNATIONAL VISUAL COMMUNICATION ASSOCIATION (IVCA)

5–6 Clipstone St
London W1P 8LD

Represents organisations and individuals working in the field of corporate video and multimedia.

MECHANICAL COPYRIGHT PROTECTION SOCIETY (MCPS)

Elgar House, 41 Streatham High Road
London SW16 1ER

Collects royalties due to music composers and publishers. Arranges licences required for use of music in productions.

PRODUCERS ALLIANCE FOR CINEMA & TELEVISION (PACT)

45 Mortimer Street
London W1N 7TP
0171-331-6000
also at
74 Victoria Crescent, Glasgow G12 9JN
0141-339-5660

Represents independent feature film and television producers and acts as a contact point for international co-production and as a link with distributors.

WRITER'S GUILD

430 Edgware Road
London W2 1EH
0171-723-8074

Union representing writers in film, television, radio, theatre and literature.

GLOSSARY

The following are some of the words and expressions that are widely used throughout the industry. Most are explained more fully elsewhere in this book. The list does not include the more common job titles. These are all listed in Chapter 2. Definitions that relate specifically to film will be found in Chapter 21.

1 inch   Linear tape format for edit mastering.

2-shot   Shot showing two people.

3-shot   Shot showing three people.

4-way split   Image made up of four separate pictures each quartering the screen.

Aspect Ratio Relative height and width of a picture. Standard TV picture has a 4:3 aspect ratio.

Aston   Make of caption generator.

Atmos   General atmospheric background sound. See also **Buzz Track**.

Autoconform Semi-automated online assembly of a program using rushes (master tapes) and time code data from an offline.

Barn Door   Hinged metal flaps around a lamp used to control where light is spilling.

Bars   Vertical colour bars recorded at the start of a tape so that it will line up with any machine it will be played on. See also **Tone**.

BCU   Big Close Up – on a person not showing much more than eyes and lips.

Beta SP Beta SP, the standard linear tape format for most broadcast news, current affairs, documentary and corporate shooting.

Betamax An early rival to VHS. Rarely found now but not to be confused with Beta SP.

BITC Burnt-in time code.

Blonde Lamp used to light medium-sized areas.

Bookends Unsatisfactory shot of two people facing one another with too much dead space between them.

Boom Microphone or lighting pole set roughly parallel to the floor supported by a vertical stand.

Build Simple animation where items build up on a graphic. Live action where items build up to form an image e.g. food items appearing one by one on a plate.

Buzz Track General background sound recorded at a location. See also **Atmos**.

Call Sheet Paperwork detailing where everyone has to be at what time for a shoot.

Cans Headphones.

Caption Text or **titling** usually naming a person superimposed on their picture. See **Name Super** and **Aston**.

Cheat To move a subject or a prop so as to improve composition of an image – usually to a position it would not normally be in. 'Cheat the flower vase over a bit'.

Chroma Colour level.

GLOSSARY

Chromakey Method of overlaying one image over part of another. The foreground image is shot against a blue or green background and a second image is keyed onto the background.

Clear Instruction to a camera on a studio shoot to move from one area to another.

Clip A shot or shots selected for viewing or inserting as part of an edit.

Clock Countdown clock recorded or edited on front of insert or program for identification purposes and for pre-roll on live transmission.

Continuity The art of making sure that details of action and props match in consecutive shots.

Crab Crabwise camera movement though an arc.

CSO Colour separation overlay. See **Chromakey**.

CU Close up shot – on a person cutting off just below the neck.

Cue Signal for someone to start speaking or moving. Usually a hand dropped just under the lens.

Cue Light Light used to cue a voice-over artist in a dubbing theatre or red light on top of a studio camera indicating it is the live camera.

Cutaway Any shot that cuts away from the main action.

Cutoff Effect of a domestic monitor cutting off the outside edge of the picture.

Cyc Continuous cyclorama made of stretched fabric or plaster around two or three sides of the studio wall – usually white but may be blue for a chromakey shoot.

Development Period of time in which a program is being devised and costed.

Digibeta High quality digital tape format.

Digitise Process of converting sound and pictures recorded in linear format to a digital format e.g. from Beta SP to media clips to be used on a digital desktop editing system.

Dingle Overhanging foliage in foreground of shot.

Diopter Lens adapter for shooting very close up.

Dock Scenery dock is where sets are stored.

Dolly Mobile platform on which camera sits to achieve tracking shots.

Downstage Area closest to the camera. See also **Upstage**.

Dropout Momentary fault on a recording. Can usually be repaired in editing.

Dry-hire Hiring a facility or equipment without people.

Drapes Large areas of fabric curtaining to create backdrop for shooting.

Dub A copy of a tape or the process of recording and mixing sound.

Dubbing Theatre Post-production facility where soundtracks are recorded and mixed.

DV Digital video – generic term for compressed digital video formats such as DVCPro, DVCam, Digital S or Beta SX.

DVE Digital video effect – may be referred to by trade name such as ADO, Abekas or Quantel.

Glossary

Edit Master   Final edited version of a program on tape.

Edit Point   The point at which an edit occurs.

Edgy   Framing is such that a subject is too close to the edge of frame.

Effects Bank   Controls and switches for generating digital video effects.

EDL   Edit decision list. Shows time codes and assembly order for all clips used in an offline.

ENG   Electronic news gathering – also a general term for tape cameras.

EQ   Equalise sound to minimise any hiss and rumble. 'Sound's a bit dodgy – we'll need to EQ it in the dub'.

Establisher   Establishing shot that sets the scene for the viewer.

Eyeline   Direction in which a person is looking relative to the camera.

Facility   Any company offering a combination of technical equipment and people.

Facility Fee   Payment for the use of a location for shooting.

Favour   Show more or a better view of one subject rather than another in the same frame.

Fill   Area on a **matte** or **chromakey** shot that fills with another image or part of it.

Fine Cut   Final offline edit of a program.

Fishpole   Hand-held pole for use with a mike.

Flag   Square or rectangular piece of black metal on its own stand used to deflect or mask light.

Flare   Unwanted hot light coming back at the camera.

Flat   Covered frame used as part of set.

Flip   Turn a picture upside down. See also **Flop**.

Flood   Adjust a lamp so that it is lighting as wide an area as possible.

Floor Plan   Plan of studio floor showing cabling of cameras, position of sets, etc.

Flop   Reverse a picture horizontally so that what was on the left originally is now on the right and vice versa.

Framestore   System for storing graphics so that they can be called up on cue on a studio shoot.

Freeze   Repeat an individual frame so that the action appears to freeze.

FVO   Female voice-over.

Gaffer   Chief electrician.

Gaffer Tape   White fabric-based adhesive tape that sticks to almost anything but is easily removable, easy to tear off and easy to write on.

Gallery   Control room in a studio.

Gel   Transparent coloured gel temporarily attached to barn doors of a light.

Glitch   A temporary fault.

Gnats   A tiny amount. 'Ease in a gnats' – as in gnat's whisker. So small you can't measure it but a little bit tighter than it is at the moment.

Green Room Waiting room for studio guests.

Grip Person who carries and sets up camera equipment and/or sets up and operates tracking equipment.

Guide See **Scratch commentary**. Also referred to as **guide commentary**.

Hal Digital system for achieving high-end graphic animation and editing effects.

Handles Additional frames at the start and finish of a clip to give an editor or dubbing mixer sufficient material to work with.

Headroom Space to allow in frame above a person's head – plus allowing for **cutoff**.

Hi-band Predecessor of Beta SP. Also referred to as BVU.

Hot Spot Area on the picture that is picking up or reflecting too much light.

Jib The arm of a camera crane.

Jump Cut Edit that results from removing frames from what was shot as continuous action with no change of shot size. Usually unacceptable.

Key See **Chromakey** and/or **Matte**.

Key Light The primary lamp in a lighting set up.

Knock Back Reduce light and colour levels to achieve a faded effect to the picture.

Leading Space Space in frame ahead of a moving subject.

(The) Line The line of action which should not be crossed.

Lo-band Low resolution version of Hi-band used for offline editing. Also referred to as Lo-band umatic.

Log Record of individual shots and takes with time codes and comments.

Looking Space Space in frame to one side of subject's face in direction they are looking.

LS Long shot – on a person a full length shot.

M&E Mixed music and effects soundtrack kept separate usually for foreign language versions.

Mask To hide or obscure. 'Cheat him camera left a gnats – his right – he's going to be masked by the person in the foreground'.

Master Shot Shot showing a complete action. Governs how everything should look in all other shots of the same scene.

Matte A black and white cutout of an image – usually a graphic. Two images can then be keyed separately onto the black or white areas of the matte.

MCU Medium close up – on a person cutting off at breast- pocket level.

Mix One image fades away as another fades in. Also known as a dissolve or cross fade.

MS Mid shot – on a person cutting off at the waist.

MLS Medium long shot – on a person cutting off around the knee.

Motion Control Computerised system for controlling all camera movement e.g. as part of rostrum camera set up, scale model shoots, etc.

GLOSSARY

Multi-layering Combining two or more picture sources simultaneously to produce a final image.

MVO Male voice-over.

Name Super Caption naming a person superimposed over their picture.

NLB No lunch break.

Noddy Mute shot of a reporter nodding in response to an interviewee.

Noisy A colour that breaks up on tape. Primary red is usually noisy by the time it gets to VHS.

Non-sync Where sound and picture were not recorded synchronously. A voice-over is non-sync. See also **Wild**.

NTSC Television standard system for the United States and Japan.

Offline Edit First low resolution assembly of a program.

Online Edit Final high resolution assembly of program at which visual effects and captions are added to produce edit master.

Paintbox Trade name often used to refer to any computer graphics system.

PAL Television standard system developed in Great Britain where it is the standard. Also the standard in much of western Europe and former British colonies.

Pan Shot achieved by the camera traversing either left or right.

Pass One or any number of times you may need to run an individual edit and copy and re-copy to achieve a complex video effect if you do not have sufficient play-in machines or effects channels.

Pick-up Point in a script at which a line of dialogue is picked up after a break in recording.

Post-production Period of time in which program is being edited and finished.

POV Point of view – where camera shoots from a subject's point of view.

Practical A household light switch or lamp.

Pre-production Period of time in which a program is being planned and scheduled.

Pre-roll Number of seconds a **VT** clip needs to be backed off from the start before it is run on a live transmission.

Preview View a picture source or clip before it is transmitted or edited.

Production Period of time in which material is being shot or acquired.

Project List of commands and time code data held in a computer file relating to a digital desktop edit.

Props Short for property. Any inanimate object that is not part of the set but which will appear on camera. Also short for properties buyer.

Racks Vision control independent of the camera operator.

Recce To inspect a location or studio prior to shooting. Pronounced recky.

Redhead Lamp used for interviews and lighting relatively small areas.

Reflector Board Silvered board or stretched material used to reflect sunlight.

Register Exactly the same size and in exactly the same position as a preceding image. Graphics that build need to be in register. If they are not you will see a **shift** or slight movement at an **edit point**.

Render Process of colouring up and transferring computer graphic animation frame by frame to tape. Also process in digital desktop online involving completion of video effects.

Reverse Angle Shot taken from the opposite angle to the previous shot or master shot.

Rostrum Camera Fixed camera used to shoot stills and artwork.

Rough Preliminary sketch of a graphic or illustration.

Rough Cut First edit of a program.

Rushes First generation tapes on which material has been shot.

Running Order Paperwork showing the order of items in a live or 'as live' program, their sources, presenters, etc.

RV Rendezvous point – where everyone should meet up. Should be shown on the **call sheet**.

Scanner Mobile control room on an outside broadcast.

Scratch Commentary Voice-over recorded by someone other than the program narrator for offline editing purposes. Also known as a **guide**.

Scrim Material attached to barn doors of a lamp to soften effect of lighting.

SCUM Single Camera Unit Midlands. (This acronym was abandoned once the administrator responsible for dreaming it up realised what it spelled).

SECAM Television standard system developed in France where it is the standard. Also the standard for Russia, much of eastern Europe and the former French colonies.

SFX Sound effects.

Sharp In focus.

Shift Movement you don't want on an edit. Occurs because you are trying to join two shots that are almost but not quite identical. See also **register**.

Showreel Compilation of examples of work for showing to potential clients.

Single A shot showing one person.

Soft Out of focus.

Spark Lighting electrician.

Split Edit Sound and picture edit where outgoing sync sound and incoming picture overlap.

Spot To narrow the focus of a light. Opposite of **flood**.

Spot Effect Sound effect either off disk or specially created. Added either at edit or dub.

Standards Conversion The process of converting tapes from one television system to another e.g. from PAL to NTSC.

Static Shot where there is no lens or camera movement.

Glossary

Still   Still photograph or illustration.

Stock   Unexposed film or fresh tape.

Strike   To remove props, set or items of equipment no longer required.

Switch Talkback   Talkback that only operates when a switch is held down by the user.

Sync   Synchronous sound and picture both recorded simultaneously.

Talkback   Intercom system used for communication between gallery and studio.

Time Code   System for numbering and identifying individual frames.

Timeline   Visual reference showing video and sound tracks, clips and edit points in a digital desktop edit.

Titles   The opening sequence of a program.

Titling   See **Caption**.

Title Safe   Area of the screen in which it is safe to run text without fear of cutoff.

Tone   High pitched continuous sound used for lining up tapes and playback or recording equipment.

Track   Camera movement where the camera itself moves in relation to a subject. Also means the track on which the dolly is travelling and is abbreviation for Soundtrack.

Transfers   Copies of rushes on lower quality stock e.g. from Beta SP to VHS.

Treatment Document outlining a program proposal and its creative treatment.

TX Transmission – as in **TX Monitor** – monitor showing studio output selected for transmission.

Umatic See **Hi-band** and **Lo-band**.

Upstage Area furthest away from the camera. Opposite of **Downstage**.

Victim Interviewee.

VO Voice-over.

VT or VTR Video tape recorder.

WA Wide angle.

White balance Method of ensuring the camera is adjusted to ambient light and colour conditions by showing it a white sheet of paper or white material.

Wild Non-sync sound – hence **wildtrack**.

Wipe Two-dimensional effect revealing one picture from behind another by means of a vertical, horizontal, diagonal or geometrically shaped wipe.

Working Title Reference title given to a production and used before its actual title is decided upon.

Wrap To complete shooting at a location, for the day or for the production.

Now see if you can translate this:

'The call was for 8 but no one had given the spark the RV. We couldn't do a white balance till he'd turned up with the redheads. The grip hadn't greased his dolly. Sound couldn't generate any tone. So we shot it all mute in long shot plus a load of noddies. They're off to record a wildtrack now and try and sync it all up in the dub. Continuity was all over the place so they're going to have a hell of a time in the offline. After we'd wrapped the director told me he'll be able to chromakey in a load of different backgrounds. Still, not my problem. You putting in for an NLB?'

INDEX

www.focalpress.com

Visit our web site for:
- the latest information on new and forthcoming Focal Press titles
- special offers
- our e-mail news service

Join our Focal Press Bookbuyers' Club

As a member, you will enjoy the following benefits:
- special discounts on new and best-selling titles
- advance information on forthcoming Focal Press books
- a quarterly newsletter highlighting special offers
- a 30-day guarantee on purchased titles

Membership is free. To join, supply your name, company, address, telephone/fax numbers and e-mail address to:
Claire Johnston
E-mail: claire.johnston@repp.co.uk
Fax: +44(0) 1865 314572
Address: Focal Press, Linacre House, Jordan Hill, Oxford OX2 8DP

Catalogue

For information on all Focal Press titles, we will be happy to send you a free copy of the Focal Press Catalogue.

Tel: 01865 314693
E-mail: carol.burgess@repp.co.uk

Potential authors

If you have an idea for a book, please get in touch:

Europe
Beth Howard, Editorial Assistant
E-mail: beth.howard@repp.co.uk
Tel: +44 (0) 1865 314365
Fax: +44 (0) 1865 314572

USA
Marie Lee, Publisher
E-mail: marie.lee@bhusa.com
Tel: 781 904 2500
Fax: 781 904 2620